WE DESERVE TO EXIST
AN INKED ANTHOLOGY

Edited by
DAKOTA RAYNE

Copyright © 2022 by Inked in Gray

All rights reserved.

No part of this book may be reproduced in any form or by any electronic or mechanical means, including information storage and retrieval systems, without written permission from the author, except for the use of brief quotations in a book review.

The world has mistaken human rights for privilege. We must demand our right to exist without being subject to oppression, discrimination, hate, and murder.

We deserve to exist.

CONTENTS

THE LAST FLAME Marisca Pichette	1
Marisca Pichette	5
OUR LADY OF SILENCE Christina Ladd	7
Christina Ladd	13
PEOPLE LIKE US Jennifer Lee Rossman	15
Jennifer Lee Rossman	33
HUNAHPU Claudia Recinos	35
Claudia Recinos	39
AN APOLOGY TO LIGHT Emmie Christie	41
Emmie Christie	49
WHISPERED NAVAJO Bernardo Villela	51
Bernardo Villela	69
HELL OF A MIND, HEAVEN OF A MIND Rashmi Agrawal	71
Rashmi Agrawal	87
BONE MOTHER Daphne Fama	89
Daphne Fama	99
SLEEP TIGHT Tyler Wittkofsky	101
Tyler Wittkofsky	133
THE FOUR Akua Lezli Hope	135
Akua Lezli Hope	143

NO MOTHER OF FRANKENSTEIN Tessa Hastjarjanto	145
Tessa Hastjarjanto	153
DEPRESSION IN THE BACKSEAT Joris Filipp	155
Joris Filipp	171
A DAWN LESS DARK Kevin Mack	173
Kevin Mack	191
WHAT REMAINS Allison Baggott-Rowe M.A.	193
Allison Baggott-Rowe M.A.	209
Afterword	211
About the Editor	213

THE LAST FLAME
MARISCA PICHETTE

Inside a box inside a box inside a box there is a tiny wisp of prenatal flame. It has not been ignited, yet.

It stands for some neutered passion. It stands for when someone said *NO*. It stands for a hand, pulling back. It stands there so that violence can never be forgotten. It stands to remind us not to erase.

Even if it's easy.

Even if we want to.

Even if everyone else already has.

Inactive, the flame is waiting. There is no air inside the box. The box seals it in, pins it down like a butterfly on a card. The box isolates, interrogates. The box has eyes.

What would happen if we cracked open the box? What would happen if all the insides came spilling out over the grass and the little neutered flame tumbled headlong into a mass of leaves?

Air imbues it with life. Fresh fire crackles at its edges. The old enmity roars and blackens our faces with soot. The light of this awakened flame is searing, blinding. Heat makes it impossible to watch, and we look away, afraid of what is being freed.

When the box breaks in the center of the inferno, the flame hits its climax. It burns brightly before dissolving into ashes, a sudden and disappointing display. After the sparks have faded from our eyes, there is nothing to see but a broken box and a pile of ash. The wind blows it all away along with the leaves.

Those of us who have felt the flame didn't want to feel it again. We closed it in hundreds of boxes like the one it had resided in, buried it deep in cellars and museum archival shelves. Dust was a blanket to muffle its light.

But those who had never felt the flame — whose lives were cool and free of fire — with soft, baby-fresh skin ash and soot had never begrimed, unscarred cheeks and unmarked wrists; they did not want to see the flame either. Its heat and brightness scared them even more than it scared us. For a fear of the unknown is ever more potent than a fear of memory.

They did not open the box like we did.

They were afraid of what it meant for them.

When the flame consumed itself, we dusted the ash from our hands and walked away. But the light memory in our irises burned forever after, a constant reminder of what we'd seen. A visual scar watermarking every day.

The unburned ones got off easy. With no flame, no ash to recall, they let the soft awareness of what we'd endured slide from their minds like leaves over sidewalks. They moved on in their lightless lives, unable to comprehend why some of us played with fire and got burned.

One day, curiosity gets the better of them, and they walk into a museum and stand before the case that holds the flame. They don't open it, but instead pull a box of matches from their pocket. Standing in the grip of flickering fluorescents they strike a single match to see how the flame dances above their fingers.

Before there is enough smoke to smell what we have smelled, before the fire touches their fingers as we were touched, they toss the match away, still burning, onto the tile floor.

Their footsteps echo on the way out, ever louder than ours.

MARISCA PICHETTE

Marisca Pichette is a bisexual author of speculative fiction, nonfiction, and poetry. Her work has been published and is forthcoming in PseudoPod, Strange Horizons, Daily Science Fiction, Fireside, Uncharted, and PodCastle, among others. A lover of moss and monsters, she lives in Western Massachusetts. You can find her on her website, Twitter, and Instagram.

Website: mariscapichette.com

Twitter: @MariscaPichette

Instagram: @marisca_write

OUR LADY OF SILENCE
CHRISTINA LADD

Once upon a time there was a lady who loved quiet. Ever since childhood she had despised the jabber-jibe-slurp of feasts and the clang-scrape-bang of the marketplace and liked nowhere better than her thick-walled bedroom, ashes cold in the hearth, thick blankets piled atop even her head. The only other place that did not make her fractious were the temples, and many — including herself — mistook her relief for devotion.

When she came of age, she did not wish to join the chatter-clatter-screech of another household. Her father was kind, and although she was the first daughter, he allowed her to become a vestal and married off her younger sister in her stead.

Gratitude made her fervent, and she traveled to the vestalry in a haze of prayer so profound she barely noticed the jangle-clop-swish of the carriage. She even tolerated the greetings and clamor of arrival. But once her days were arranged and her mind settled, she realized: the vestalry was no haven at all.

The walls were as thin as the blankets. The fire crack-sizzle-popped, the other nuns wheedle-nag-bickered, and the wind just *moaned*. Oh, how it moaned! Like a dying man on a battlefield, now shrieking, now muttering, and always setting the stiff limbs of the trees to shudder and clack against one another.

No one else seemed to notice these noises. But to the lady, they crawled up her neck, itched under her fingernails, and stabbed and stabbed at the flesh of her mind. Worse was the feeling in her shoulders, a knot drawn ever-tighter as she began to brace herself constantly against the barrage of noises, waiting even in the hush for some unexpected sound to ruin her brief peace.

She redoubled her devotions. *Let me ignore these simple things as others do.* But no matter to which god she addressed her plea, there was no reply.

Silence. What an irony!

Try as she might, she could find no humor in it.

The lady became irritable, and then deranged. She entered rooms only to forget why she had come and left meals after only a few bites, her appetite lost. Even devotions and rituals lost their appeal, the soothing predictability of call and response mangled by the whisper-jostle-rustle of her fellow vestals. She ground her teeth at night. Sometimes the sound would wake her, her whole body shuddering as she suppressed the only noise she could, the sound of her own weeping.

One night, exhausted and awake, she gave in to the overwhelming despair. Her days were punctuated by unavoidable noise; her nights betrayed her. The only prayer she could manage was *please*.

Please.

Please.

She focused all her misery and need into the word. And in her mind, the word became a scream that drowned out the incessant wind, the midnight gossip, and all the skittering, creaking sounds of the nunnery.

Then something happened to her inward scream. It warped. It turned inside out. It became, in its sound-not-sound, a deep silence.

Shadows poured down around her like her tears. And she became afraid as she watched a figure arise from the pool of darkness, a hooded figure like all the nuns, but terribly tall and wide.

I am the goddess of silence, said the shadowy figure, and the lady turned liquid with relief. All this time, she had been praying to the wrong gods!

The goddess continued to stand over her bed, but now the lady felt safe enough to rest. Filled with a deep, rippling bliss, the lady slept through the night.

A COUGH WOKE HER, a hacking cough soggy with phlegm. She briefly wished to die. But then, from that deeply shadowed place inside her, silence flowed outward. It did not drown out the coughing, or the burst of argument from the privy down the hall, but it comforted her enough to loosen the knot of her shoulders.

All through that day, when sounds raked her, the silence rushed in like a salve. All through the next night, the shadows pressed closer to swathe her and muffle the world away. The silences began to thrill her like sweet, heady wine. She smiled. She breathed deeply. And eventually, she went before the head of the nunnery.

— I have discovered my patroness, she said. I worship the Lady of Silence. I now request a hermitage to better serve Her.

The prioress furrowed her brow.

— Who? she asked.

. . .

THEY CAME TO HER LATER, the prioress and the heads of other local nunneries and shrines. It was a cough-harumph-proclaim little crowd, their vestments redolent with scent and jewels.

— No one else has seen this goddess, they said.

— Or heard of her, one added, to the general amusement. The lady glared at them until they stopped snickering.

— There are many minor gods, though. Many aspects of the great ones, too. Is there not some sign you can show us, some mark or miracle?

— Yes, some act or vision worthy of acclaim.

They demanded proof in loud voices, a spectacle that would only inspire further chatter. She decided to pray as they continued to prattle, and soon was enveloped in the thick, shimmering peace. Their voices faded-faded-faded.

— Until there is another revelation, we will not support your hermitage, they eventually told her, but the silence cushioned their words.

The lady said nothing, and eventually the crowd went away. *It does not matter.* She did not need the vestalry. Her family had resources, connections. And even if they balked, she would find a way. She needed only the Lady.

ONCE AGAIN, she went begging to her father. But this time, purpose gave her confidence and the Goddess gave her comfort. She would not remain in the bustle-yammer-shriek household or city forever. Somehow or other, she would have her hermitage.

And so she did, but in reluctant time and with stinting supply. A vestal daughter was an honor; a hermitess was an oddity. And a devotee to an unknown goddess . . . well. Her father granted her the supplies, but told her she would have to construct the hermitage herself. Sending builders into the wilderness was too costly to his pocketbook and to his reputation. He thought she would refuse. She only hired a wagon.

The work was far more difficult than she had imagined. Her knees ached from bending and her back ached from standing. Her fingers were numb from all the tasks she had to do merely to stay alive. But she could do it in silence, and that was all she truly required.

Eventually, people began to hear rumor of the strange lady who worshipped a new goddess. A few sought her out, hesitant but curious. No authorities recognized them, but this lady and her goddess made no demands of them or of any others.

Most found it strange, but to a few it was a rare gift. The secrets they could not yet bring themselves to speak, the sorrows that had no words, all these and more the lady accepted from her visitors. Some would come to sit with her, others to work alongside her. A few even brought offerings, measures of grain and salt and cloth.

Even with occasional charity, hard living took its toll. All too soon, the lady's body crack-creak-groaned as she made her way slow and slower through her daily devotions. But although she bowed to age, she did not resent it. Time was silent, and therefore a friend.

The lady's life softened under the steady flow of silences, and when her end came, she welcomed it as she had welcomed penitents. It happened in the night. Her heart stuttered. Her breathing went from shallow to gasp-gasp-gasp. Gasp-gasp. Gasp.

Silence.

As the lady died, the shadows parted like thick curtains, and she beheld a door. The door was a mirror in which she saw her own reflection, not old and gasping, but tall and proud. The lady stepped through the mirror. The velvet shadows closed around her like a cape, and settled upon her brow like a crown. The space she had prepared for a goddess was the space she now stepped into.

The Lady of Silence reigned at last.

CHRISTINA LADD

Christina Ladd (she/her) is a writer, reviewer, and librarian who lives in Boston. She will eventually die crushed under a pile of books, but until then she survives on a worrisome amount of tea and pizza. You can find more of her work in Vastarien, A Coup of Owls, Strange Horizons and more, or on Twitter.

Twitter: @OLaddieGirl

PEOPLE LIKE US
JENNIFER LEE ROSSMAN

Millions have died. Maybe billions. I don't know; ever since the Internet went down, it's hard to keep track.

My point is, the body count is unimaginably high already. And if you're up to it, I'll help you make it a little higher.

I can't promise it will be painless, I can't even promise you'll survive it. But I can promise you this: I will do everything in my power to bring you back from the other side in the body you were meant to have.

So, what do you say? Are you up for a post-apocalyptic road trip to hell?

Don't worry. There'll be snacks.

I ALWAYS FORGET how gray it is when I come back from the underworld.

The world used to have color, didn't it? Not just in the spirits of my people. In the real world. Green leaves, blue skies, bright red lipstick. Rainbows. I couldn't have imagined rainbows.

I don't know what kind of magic they used, or even who *they* are, but they didn't just kill us. They killed our hope.

Persephone doesn't seem to have noticed the gray. She trots alongside me, happy as ever, tongue lolling and stubby little Doberman tail wagging as we cross the river. Sometimes I envy her. She doesn't see just how much joy we've lost. And she doesn't care. So long as she has me, our beat up old used-to-be-red Honda Odyssey, and a glove box full of Twinkies, she's a happy doggo.

She doesn't even mind the dead bodies.

Which reminds me . . . I look at my watch. Damn. The trip back took longer than I anticipated.

I run through the barren landscape as fast as my tired legs will allow, but I don't get to my car in time. He's already woken up and seen the body.

"Shit. I'm sorry, dude," I say, wrapping up the shaking man in a hug. "Different dimensions, scrambled time. I'm sorry you had to see that."

He doesn't say anything, just stares at the crumbling cityscape on the horizon and lets his hand find the top of Persephone's head, that soft fur right between her floppy ears.

I wish I could help him more, help guide him through this new life. But I got his spirit back in one piece, safely installed in a new body that will hide his shine from the bad people. I did my job. All I can do now is help him bury his old life.

WE DON'T USE a grave marker. Too risky. But the whole desert is a cemetery; I dread the day I forget where I've buried them all and dig a grave on top of a grave.

His funeral is simple. Just a hole in the ground, a blanket wrapped around the empty shell of his former person. Nutrition for the ground and all the critters in it.

It's sad. It's somber. But it's also a celebration. He is saying goodbye to the last physical thing keeping him from being himself.

It isn't society or hormones or body image holding him back anymore. Now, his happiness is up to him.

I offer him a ride, but he wants to sit here for a little longer. I get that. There's a lot of things to say goodbye to. So I give him a hug, and my dog and I walk back to the car under a vibrant gray sunset.

Persephone senses it before I do, tensing up beside me, her movements slow and stiff with caution. I think I'm just too tired, my soul exhausted from the trip. I don't see it until we're just a few yards from the car, but it is unmistakable: a rainbow glow. An aura.

My next client.

"Look," I say. "I'm not in any form to take another trip right now. I'll get you what you need, but we have to wait until tomorrow—"

It's a kid.

I come to a complete stop, but Persephone has apparently deemed them harmless and bounds ahead, lavishing them in doggy kisses.

I hate when it's kids. I hate how alone they are, how brightly they glow. This kid is a Technicolor denizen of Oz trapped in a monochrome Kansas. It's a wonder they've lasted this long, and it's only a matter of time until the flying monkeys catch up to them. No way can this wait until tomorrow.

Fuck.

"I THOUGHT you just came from the other side. Why do we have to drive somewhere else?" the child asks.

This is another reason I hate when it's kids. They ask questions I don't have the answers to. It's also why I love them so much.

"It's complicated. The ferryman isn't always working the same port."

Max frowns. "Port?"

"It's a Greek mythology metaphor," I explain, twirling my lucky coin between my fingers as I drive. Nervous habit. "The River Styx, Charon ferrying people from the realm of the living to the realm of the dead . . . It's what I say because I don't know why sometimes I can cross over and sometimes I can't. It's like . . . I don't know . . . . The veil between worlds gets thinner in certain places at certain times, and there's no real pattern. I just follow the feeling."

The kid nods slowly, slipping a piece of snack cake to Persephone in the backseat. I pretend not to notice.

Ghostly gray shapes flick past the windows as we drive through the darkness of the desert. Just rock formations and the odd cactus, I tell myself. If it was anything more sinister, they would have gotten us by now anyway.

"So. What pronouns do you want me to use for you? Because I use they/them for everyone until I'm sure what they like."

Max considers this for a moment, playing with the hem of

their dress. Pink. No, magenta. I try not to stare, but I haven't seen such vibrant shades in a long time. I had forgotten the upholstery of my car used to be cream, not white, but everything in Max's vicinity suddenly remembers what it used to be. It's such a simple thing, color, but absolutely breathtaking.

"I can be a they?"

The pure hope in their tiny, scared voice tightens my throat with tears. This is the moment they realize it's perfectly all right to check the gender box marked "C, none of the above."

"Yeah, kid." I wipe my eyes, muttering something about desert dust. "Yeah. You can be a they. You can be whatever you need to be."

I tighten the grip on my steering wheel as the broken skyline draws nearer.

"And right now, I need you to be brave."

"Do you know what they are? The bad things? Do you know where they come from?"

More questions I don't have answers to. I shake my head and take Max's hand. For a second, I forget the mission, too transfixed by my own skin tone. Darker than I remember. Must be getting tan in the sun.

"Sorry, what?" I ask as we follow Persephone through the shadows of crumbling buildings and abandoned vehicles.

"What are they?" Max reiterates. "How did they make the world so sad?"

I do a little bit of mental math. Max looks to be about ten . . . . . So yeah. They would've been five or six when marginalized people started disappearing, when those things came and drained the color from the world. Too young to have been watching the news.

Not like that would have helped them. The news had no clue what was happening. None of us did.

"I don't know, kid." I resist the urge to whisper. My instincts tell me to keep quiet, but that doesn't matter. The things find you no matter what. "Aliens, fairies, inter-dimensional assholes. I don't know what they are, and I don't care. All I know is they get rid of anything that doesn't go along with their twisted idea of normal. Us queers were some of the first to go, but they doubly want me gone because I've got magic on my side."

Footsteps catch my attention somewhere to my left. More survivors — invaders don't make sound.

Max presses themself against my side, their hand never leaving Persephone's back.

"It's okay, kid. It's just people, like us." I reconsider. "Not *like us*, like us. They aren't queer. But they're people nonetheless, caught in the crossfire of this hateful genocide against those who sparkle."

Well, they might be queer. They might be disabled or autistic or gay or any of the thousand things the invaders want to eradicate.

"They don't have gender dysphoria. I know they don't, because I can't see them glowing." It's an oversimplification, though. But I think right now, the kid needs the world to be simple.

We come to a part of the city that has survived more or less unscathed. No electricity, no cars. But something resembling civilization still lives on here. Houses and scavenger markets . . . and a hospital, which is our destination. It's a different kind of life, but it's life nonetheless.

Lamps glow softly in the windows of the two-story brick

affair, defiantly refusing to let night fall. A beautiful sight, even if the flames are gray and white instead of vibrant orange and red.

The kid hesitates in the doorway of the hospital. "What are we doing here? Is this where the ferry is waiting?"

I take a deep breath. "No. This is where we find your new body."

THEY WON'T CHOOSE ONE. I'm trying not to show my impatience, but I risk a lot to bring people to this morgue, and Persephone is whining in the doorway and it's only a matter of time until someone finds us.

"I know it's hard, kid," I say quietly. "It's never easy to look at bodies. Especially when they're your age —"

"It's not that." Max frowns and looks up at me. "I like my body. Why do I need a new one?"

Huh. No one has ever asked that before. Ever. Why would someone not want a new body if the one they were born with doesn't match who they are on the inside?

I loved my old body. It served me well. But my new one . . . It has curves where I want them and no curves where I don't. It produces the right hormones. *It is me.* And I think everyone else who has gone with me to hell and back would agree — they tell me they feel whole for the first time in their lives, and the painful glowing fades when they are in a body that fits.

I lean back on the wall of the morgue. The kid has me flummoxed. I don't know how to help them if they don't want to die and be reborn into another, more suitable body. That's what I do. That's how I help.

Persephone whines, shifting her weight from side to side and growing restless.

"Max," I say to the rainbow child in the gray and black darkness. "I don't know what to tell you. We don't have a lot of options here, kid. The things . . . they see you as the enemy, but they can only see you because you glow. I think your glow is beautiful, but it is dangerous. It will get you noticed, and getting noticed will get you killed. Pick a body you feel comfortable in, the dysphoria goes away, and so does the glow."

Still, they hesitate.

"The glow comes from a place of pain, but we can fix it." Except Max doesn't seem to be suffering in their body, not like I was. "Don't you feel pain, being the way you are? Isn't that why you came to me?"

They nod. "But I don't know what a they looks like. Or what it feels like to be one. Why can't it look like me?"

They're right. I hate it, but they're right.

No, I love it. I love that they are comfortable in their own body. But then why are they in color?

Persephone barks. The things are coming. *Shit.*

"Are you sure?" I ask Max. They nod. I take their hand and we run. I don't know where, just . . . away.

THE THINGS . . . the others . . . the invaders. Whatever you want to call them. I've never actually seen one before. Just heard rumors, warnings. I guess anyone who's seen them probably hasn't lived to tell.

Here's to hoping we're the exception.

Humans. They look like humans. Somehow even more

colorless than the rest of us like their very existence is leeching joy from the world.

They drive cars. Or at least, these two do. A sleek, shiny sports car. Black, with gray accents, just like their suits.

Maybe they are human. Maybe we did this to ourselves. But it's not like it matters. Whatever they are, they're not going to stop killing the people who don't conform to their version of what reality should be.

I try not to look at the gas gauge, but the needle is hovering near the E, and I don't think it stands for Enough. Endless, maybe, like the desert around us. A never-ending graveyard with no escape.

I glance at Max. The kaleidoscope kid is clearly terrified, but they're trying not to let it show.

"We'll be okay," I lie. Or maybe I'm not lying. I don't really know yet, but my mind is spinning, desperately reaching for any way out of this. If I can find an entrance to the underworld . . .

"I like my body," Max says softly. "But I don't like that other people don't like it. Does that make sense?"

"Yeah, kid. It does."

"Before today. Before I knew I could be a they like you, I didn't fit in. People want me to be a boy like my parents always thought I was, or they want me to be a girl because I like wearing dresses. Sometimes I wish my face was a girl face, and sometimes I wish I could grow up and fit into my dresses better. But I think I want to grow a beard someday, and I think it would be hard to put on a bra."

Well, they're right about that.

"I don't want a new body. I want other people to think *this* is the right body for me, even if that means I can't hide."

"Passing," I say, finally understanding. "You're talking about passing. When you're non-binary, sometimes the way you want to look and act and feel doesn't fit in with what society thinks about genders. Sometimes you can get away with people thinking you're a boy or a girl, and that's called passing and it's awesome for some people who want to pass, but we don't all want that and some of us can't have it."

I'm rambling, I know I am. But I'm on the verge of something. Exhilaration builds up inside of me.

I've met people with dysphoria so bad it made them unbearably depressed and desperate, and they weren't nearly as brightly colored as Max. And Max is the first person I've met in this apocalypse who is comfortable enough in their own body to risk not passing. So what if . . .

Oh, I don't even want to say it in case I'm wrong. But what if their glow, their colors, what if that isn't pain? What if it's confidence? Gender . . . euphoria? I can barely breathe. This feels big, but what can I do with that information?

A sharp bark from the backseat. Yeah. Now that Persephone mentions it, I do feel a portal, a place where the ferry is docked. I squeeze my lucky coin so tight, my knuckles turn white. Well, whiter. "Kid?"

"Yeah?"

"I've got an idea. It's not a good one, but it's the only one we've got at the moment."

" . . . What is it?"

"We stop hiding, and start fighting back."

Max doesn't respond right away, anxiously devoting all of their attention to unwrapping a snack.

"Look. I get it. This is the way things have been for so long, and it's scary to change, even if the change will be for the better in the end. But if you trust me for a little while longer, I promise you everything will be okay." I'm not sure if that's a promise I can even make, but I extend my hand across the center console anyway. "What do you say, kid?"

After a moment's deliberation, Max shakes my hand. I think I see a little bit of hope in their smile, and when they take their hand away, a little bit of color radiates up my arm.

I don't know what Max sees as we cross the River Styx. Every person sees something different. Most see whatever they think the entrance to hell looks like, a couple fantasy nerds have seen the gates to the Mines of Moria, one woman told me it looks like the intro to *The Twilight Zone*.

I don't actually see a river, that's just a metaphor. I see a tunnel cut into the side of a mountain. Dark, foreboding, only a tiny pinprick of light to suggest another side even exists.

Every time I go through, I worry that this will be the time I don't want to come out.

I squeeze Max's hand as we speed toward the mountain. "This is going to be a little different than my usual crossings. But we're going to be fine. I just need you to remember one thing, all right? We can't stay. No matter how good it seems, no matter how much better it is than up here, it is not our time. Someday, yeah. But we got lives to live before we come back here for good."

I press my lucky coin to my lips, and we enter the tunnel.

I've lost track of how many times I've died. I don't even feel my spirit being torn from my body anymore. Persephone . . . Well, dogs are different. A little more divine than us humans; this is nothing for her.

Max, though. They feel it.

"I don't like this," they whisper.

I wrap my arm around their shoulders, pull them in tight. "Weird, right? Like you know it hurts, like it's the worst pain you've ever felt, but you can't actually feel it?"

"I don't like it," they say again. They glance behind us, but there's nothing there except golden desert. "Are we dead?"

"Kind of."

I take a moment to find my bearings, remember how to breathe again. It's always hard to remember that I can take my time, that only a few seconds should pass by the time we get out of here. The things chasing us should never even notice that I was briefly unconscious — well, soulless, really — behind the wheel. So long as I don't lose track of time.

"You ever see cartoons? The old ones with Bugs Bunny and all them?"

Max scrunches up their face in thought. "I think so?"

"All right, you know how, when a cartoon character dies, their soul floats above them for a little while, and then it can go back into the body instead of going to Heaven? That's what we're doing right now. We are technically dead, and we have left our bodies and gone to the afterlife, but we're not *dead-dead*. We're going back."

"I thought we were coming here to escape?" they ask, following along in confusion as Persephone and I lead them along a well-worn path. The sand is packed down hard, compressed so much it almost glitters like diamonds. It's too beautiful here, too tempting.

"Not escape," I correct. "We're just getting reinforcements."

A city appears over the horizon, and all of a sudden we're there. No time wasted, like a dream that cuts out the boring bits.

The city towers over us, an impossible MC Escher drawing painted by Lisa Frank — buildings and trees and monuments stretching and dancing toward a sky of daylight aurora borealis. And all around and in the city: people. Spirits so bright and diaphanous they almost hurt my eyes.

Max takes my hand again. "Our reinforcements . . . are ghosts?" they whisper.

"No. Not quite. Our reinforcements are all the people up there in the real world, the ones trying to hide their glow so the things won't take them. But yeah. We're using the ghosts."

From the top of the highest tower in the underworld, we can see forever. Perfection, paradise, everything a desperate soul could ever want. So I tell Max not to look, because I can't risk them wanting to stay. I can't go back alone, not again, not this time.

"How does it work?" they ask, staring at me instead of out the windows, showing great restraint. I always look.

"You ever have an idea come from nowhere? Just randomly think of something you never would have thought of, and it ends up being something great?"

They nod. "Like when you . . ." They hesitate. "That *was* you, wasn't it? The message?"

"Yeah, kid. That was me." I take a deep breath, pull my hair back, close my eyes. The veil between the worlds is thin here; easy to pierce. That doesn't mean it doesn't take a lot of energy.

I twirl my lucky coin in my hand, focusing on the rhythm of my fingers until the motion becomes like a metronome to calm my frantic mind.

Focus. Breathe. Talk to the spirits.

"We need your help."

Honestly, I'm not sure whether I'm talking out loud or just in my head. I've never done it around another living soul before. Either way, I imagine my words projected out across the underworld like a broadcast from a radio tower, beaming out to all who will listen.

"I need you to go out there. Out into the world of the living again. I need you to carry a message to everyone you encounter, plant this seed of an idea in their heads. In their hearts."

Deep breath. Focus all of my nervous energy on this moment.

"Millions, maybe billions of people have died. There's no changing that, and I bet a lot of you have thought about joining the death toll in one way or another. I've dedicated my life to helping people like us go to the underworld and come back in the body you were meant to have. And if this doesn't work, I will continue to do that until the day I don't have a return ticket. Hell, even if this does work, I'll still help those of you who want a new body."

The irony of saying "hell" in the actual afterlife strikes me as funny, but I can't laugh. If I laugh, I'm afraid I will start crying.

"Hiding is good. Hiding keeps us alive. But being alive is not the same as living. What I'm about to say won't ring true for all of you, and that's okay. Everyone's gotta do this their own way, the way that works for them."

I take another deep breath, try to find the courage to start a revolution.

"I see you. The people with the pain so bad, you shine like a beacon in the gray. The flesh and bones and hormones that make up your body don't fit with what you feel inside. So you try to change your body. Or maybe you change yourself to fit your body. And maybe that works for you, but there are some of us who don't want to hide, for whom the perfect body doesn't exist. Those are the people I'm talking to."

Max takes my hand, and I open my eyes to look at them. Warm tan skin, rosy lips, eyes golden green. So many colors.

"I'm talking to the hes who wear heels and run on estrogen. The shes with strong jawlines and deep voices. The theys and the xies and the zirs and the people whose pronouns change and those who don't even have a gender. You are beautiful. You are amazing. You looked at the status quo and you said *nope, not for me*. You carved out your place in this world, and your body may not be perfect for you, but it is still perfect because it *is* you. And I know it's hard sometimes to love it, but I need you to try. Just for a moment, just for me. Love yourself. Love your gender. Revel in the wondrousness that is you, and maybe we can take back this world."

I don't feel like that's enough. I should say more, shouldn't I? Max squeezes my hand again.

But words won't change anything. If it's possible, if enough people can find it in their hearts to love themselves in the face of all their dysphoria, it will work no matter what I say. I just have to give them the chance to realize it.

I send out the ghosts. It's out of my hands now.

It takes me longer than usual to find return passage. I think it is because I'm trying to find my way back to a moving vehicle, rather than the stationary place where I usually leave my body. Then again, maybe part of me doesn't want to go back because... What if it didn't work? What if the world is just as gray and miserable as always?

What if there's no hope?

But eventually, I find it. The way back home.

Max, Persephone, and I are back in our bodies, mere seconds after we left them. Time gets wonky down there, but this was a relatively short trip. Actually going through the "dying" process in order to fully detach someone from their body and prepare the soul for its new vessel... That can take what feels like days, weeks in the underworld.

We are still in the tunnel, still hurtling ahead with the others close on our tail. But the light up ahead is growing larger, closer. We're there, we've made it.

The car bursts into the sunlight, the brightness making me squint. Before my eyes can adjust, my car decides it has run on fumes long enough and dies on me.

No, not now! Not with those things right behind us.

In desperation, I flick the dashboard. Because it's clearly the fault of the fuel gauge, not the gas tank. Because I don't know what else to do. Because I have to do something.

My eyes begin to adjust to the light, and I notice something weird about my hand. I flick the dashboard again, watching my fingers curiously. They're tan. Not . . . not gray.

It's Max. Has to be. Max's color is encroaching on me again.

I look towards them. The interior of my car is a little less gray than it used to be, but there is a very clear distinction between Max's color and my own.

My color is emanating from *me*. From *my* beautiful, queer body that still isn't exactly the one I had in mind, but is still pretty damn perfect.

My glow gets a little more vibrant as the car slows to a stop. The last time I shined, it hurt so much I almost stayed in the underworld. My instinct is to despise it, but it isn't pain anymore.

Somewhere on the horizon, the sky lights up in a thin

column, like a spotlight. Just a sliver of deep blue, of purple mountains.

Another column of pink sunrise, and another. I hear the squeal of tires as the other car pulls up behind us, but it doesn't matter anymore.

I look at Max, realize they are hiding behind their hands. "Kid," I say, tapping them on the arm. "Kid, you gotta see this."

More lights go up, growing wider and spreading into one another as they sweep across the land, drenching everything in vivid color. But I'm not watching it anymore; I'm watching Max.

The look on their face is more wondrous than the event outside. It's joy, hope. It's them imagining a future, maybe even a good one, for the first time in years.

I don't want to interrupt this moment, but I think I can replace it with an even better one. "Kid," I whisper, tapping them on the arm.

They look at me, and break into a grin. "You're colorful."

"I am," I say, mirroring their grin. I nod in the general direction of outside. "Come on. Let's go end this."

The kid, my dog, and I get out of the car — the bright red steel monstrosity with burnt orange rust creeping up its sides. We stand on sand turned amber by the first rays of sunlight, defiantly watching as those hideous gray things get out of their car.

Color sweeps across the land, pulsing and growing brighter and more vivid with every person who hears our message and decides to let him/her/them/zirself believe in a world where they are accepted for who and what they are.

But no color can touch the things. They grow more and more gray, just sad old crones who ride bicycles through Kansas tornadoes, being devoured by the Technicolor wonders of Oz. When they can't get any more colorless, they start losing their contrast. No lights and shadows, just gray. Endless gray.

And then they're gone. Them, and all the things like them that tried to take our world from people like us.

I'd say they can go to hell, but I don't think they'd like it there very much. It's almost as beautiful as the world we're taking back today.

JENNIFER LEE ROSSMAN

Jennifer Lee Rossman (she/they) is a queer, disabled, and autistic author and editor from Binghamton, New York. They are a girl the same way Y is a vowel — sometimes, but not really. Follow them on Twitter and find more of their work on their website.

Website: jenniferleerossman.blogspot.com

Twitter: @JenLRossman

Hunahpu
Claudia Recinos

Hunahpu is going mad. He can feel it. His mind is fraying like a bit of maize silk. He heard someone say once that if you *think* you're going mad, you're probably not, but he can tell you from experience that that's not the case. Madness doesn't care what you think of it. Madness grabs what it wants and doesn't give a lick if it's seen.

It wasn't always this way. Hunahpu was a great Mayan god, once. The feather in his cap serves as a reminder – a great, green wisp of plumage he took from the tail of a demon bird. Hunahpu wears the feather to remind him of his heroic deeds. For centuries, it shone like a beacon. But, lately, all it does is trigger his allergies and smell vaguely of mold.

Hunahpu hugs his arms around himself. He sways back and forth like a pendulum. It's not his fault he's going crazy. He's a god, and what are gods but stories, constantly changing? Every telling alters a piece of him. Out of one mouth, he emerges as the protagonist, a benevolent hero. Out of another mouth, he crawls forth a villain. The duality is staggering. How can it not drive him to the edge?

Here is a story: Hunahpu used to be a twin, half of a set. Hunahpu's brother, the steadfast Xbalanque, saw their end coming, and in his despair, he buried himself in the dirt. Xbalanque blossoms and seeds, and falls into the soil once more. In this perpetual cycle, he lives on, no good to anybody but himself. It was a cowardly act, in Hunahpu's opinion, and he blanches each time he thinks of it. So, he doesn't. He carries on, a solitary figure. He carries on, a plot structure all his own.

But, now, he's gibbering. Now he's losing the story. He could have sworn there was someone standing there, listening. But when he turns his head, he finds only ghosts. Like the mist that gathers in the jungle each morning, sweeping over vines and black earth where his worshippers once walked. Like the steaming threads that curl over the ruins of dead civilizations, only to burn away once the great ball of the sun rises high in the sky.

Hunahpu lets out a great big puff of air and the ghosts vanish. But, then, Hunahpu is left all on his own.

Stories.

Who will hear his stories?

What is left of Hunahpu if there is no one to tell his tale?

Once, there was a man from a great land called Spain. He called himself a priest. He built a bonfire hot enough to rival the summer sun, and in a fit of pique, he burned all the old stories, Hunahpu's among them. Hunahpu can still see it—the way the flames licked the black sky and the smoke choked the moon and wiped out the stars.

And when the smoke cleared: dark bodies hanging from the walls of the new churches. Dark blood spilling forth like a fountain. His worshippers. His people.

Look at their purpled, silenced tongues.

What is left?

Centuries have passed and Hunahpu is still weeping into

mass graves. See the guns and the guerillas. See the boots caked with dried mud. See them stamp out women and children, heels on throats to drown out voices. Mayan voices. Mayan song. Mayan prayer and Mayan sacrifices.

Who will help them?

The new gods hold up their hands, pierced flesh and Mona Lisa smiles. The new gods don't speak Hunahpu's language. The new gods only stare and stare with their doll-button eyes. So Hunahpu is left, alone, to slink like a cat among the fruiting cacao trees. To slip into huts made of stone and mud and take what is offered. To scratch. To scrape. To get by.

And he gets by.

Hunahpu is going mad, but at least he's aware of it. He peers into a dormant volcano, white with ash. He hovers in the shadows and listens to the *señoras* gossiping in the main square. He blesses the fruit in the market stall. He blesses the cobble streets of the city's old quarter. He blesses the sky. He blesses himself.

He is still here, after all this time. He couldn't leave, even if he wanted to. He is native. He is indigenous. He is as ancient as time. He has lost parts of himself, sure. But like the calabash tree, he grows new limbs to replace the old. He is silent when he needs to think. He tells himself stories when he needs to hide. Yesterday he was a sunflower. The day before he was a small fish. Today is a good day, so he remembers himself. He is a god. He is a god. He is a god.

Once, there was a swarm of locusts with fair skin and hungry mouths. They came and devoured, stripping skin off bones. But they could not swallow a soul.

There are still souls here, scattered like pebbles or seeds. They are a vein of ore that creeps through the heart of the jungle. Mayan ruins. Mayan relics. But, also, Mayan song. The words still dance on the lips of the survivors. The story is still here, retold in new words. Passed down in whispers.

Once upon a time there were stone temples that reached to the sky. Their foundations remain. Secret cities. Secret lives.

The language has changed. The city has changed. Hunahpu is diminished.

But, more and more, Hunahpu's people are blinking their eyes open.

A new dawn.

A new day.

They uncover the old traditions like they're unearthing stones. They dust the old ways off and set them on a shelf. A place of pride! They reclaim them. They embrace their song as they were once forced to embrace the new gods. And, so, Hunahpu is reborn.

Once upon a time there was a god who vanquished a demon bird.

Once, in this city. Once, in this land.

Once upon a time there was a god, and his name was Hunahpu.

And thus, Hunahpu limps and dances on, a story told in rhythm.

CLAUDIA RECINOS

Claudia's work has appeared in *Fun 4 Kids in Buffalo* and *Touch: The Journal of Healing*. My YA verse novel, *To Be Maya*, is scheduled for publication December 2022 by West 44 Books. Claudia is a first generation Guatemalan American. When not writing, she can be found on a trapeze. For more information, please visit their website. You may also find them on Instagram, and Twitter.

Website: recinosseldeen.com

Twitter: @cloudyatweets

Instagram: @cloudya01

AN APOLOGY TO LIGHT
EMMIE CHRISTIE

The streetlight blinked, and Laura fell towards it.

The gravity on Planet F1SR, or "Fissure," felt like dream falling, except you never woke up from the jolt. She'd loved the sensation in the simulations on Earth; she always felt like it helped jar her out of old habits.

She landed on the road. Her feet slipped in her Converse. She hadn't had time to pull on socks or grab the key to the flashlight her husband stashed in his safe. She jumped again, higher than the limit of twenty feet. No one drove up there in the aircar lane, anyway, not at night.

He didn't patrol this area. But what if another cop picked her up? What if that cop worked with him on the force?

Laura needed a line of sight to jump, or she could fall into one of the craters off road, the ones that had given Fissure its name. The streetlight blinked below like the eye of a mythical Sphinx, all knowing, all judging. Could she ask it for forgiveness? Her heart pounded in trepidation.

Jump.

Fall.

Another flickering streetlight in the distance seemed far off in the cold. But she could jump the space between the streetlights. Those expensive lights. Fissure's cool, distant sun had to power most things, even cars, so much so that the planet had to ration it for the civilians. Pricey.

He'd kept the flashlight in a safe, had told her to light candles "to save money." He hadn't done it to keep her stuck at home, unable to travel without a light source, not with the danger of the fissures everywhere, carving deep into the planet. No, of course not.

He didn't know, though, that light scared her more than the dark.

"In that one poem about love," she'd said to Kesha as they'd cleared glasses off a booth table, "the one that said, 'the women come and go, talking of Michelangelo?' I'm one of the women. Senseless. I can't figure out where I want to be."

Kesha had balanced a tray on her knee while cleaning the ketchup on the table. She'd pursed her lips. "Sounds like that poem was written by a lonely man who didn't know how to talk to women."

Jump. Fall.

A distant engine revved in the airlane, above the physical road. Headlights cut around the corner.

No. No, please —

This is what happens when you run. You deserve this, you're ungrateful, disobedient —

Laura jumped off the highway, into the dark where the aircars couldn't follow. The fissures lay everywhere, like something huge had sliced deep into the planet. The road She jumped higher, not knowing where she'd land.

You'll die without me, you can't handle it out there, those holes, those crevices, they grab the guilty people, you know, the ones who have something to hide —

She landed on solid ground. The engine revved past and above her, in the aircar lane. The headlights descended to the physical roadside; he'd landed the aircar. A door slammed.

I'm sorry!

No, no, I don't want this, not anymore! I'm sorry, I can't!

He would kill her, running away had clinched that. She should've stayed put, stayed low, and stayed quiet. What about his job? Would he lose it? What would people say?

She was sorry. She really was. But she couldn't stay anymore. She didn't know where to go; but she knew she couldn't stay.

She jumped. 40 feet? She couldn't tell, without the light.

Falling. Falling forever.

Kesha's words fell with her. "You're responsible for you. Not for him."

"But he's on the force," Laura had said. She'd meant to delve deeper into those words, to scrape the paint away to the rot underneath, but she'd hesitated, protected his image once again. She couldn't run from a charmer, from someone who hid behind straight white teeth and deep bass voice, who said, *you're late.* The words promised punishment for later, behind closed doors, when he could slip off his mask to reveal a gaping hole of need and ice. *Say you're sorry, say it, you damn well know why —*

She landed. Tears on her cheeks, sweat in her converse. A sound to her left, the crunch of someone picking their way across the rocky ground.

She muffled her yelp with a hand over her mouth. Had he followed her?

A beam of light cut towards her. He hadn't jumped after her, but he had the flashlight, of course, and was picking his way towards her. Only crazy people jumped in the night without a light. Crazy people like her. *Shit. Shit.*

Her trembling legs refused to jump. She tried to step away with care, with finesse, but tripped on some damn rock and landed sprawled out on the rocky ground.

Footsteps. Running.

She'd shattered a vase over his head. Assaulted him. For what? Because he cared about her being home on time? Because he'd smashed her phone? He hadn't hit *her*, not ever. He'd said he would never do that. He protected and served every night. Her and her hormones. And after all he had done for her, like getting her that job at the diner? Well. Thankless. He'd asked, *have you messaged Kesha about me?* That shard of murder in his eye hadn't gleamed for her, she'd imagined it. She had no proof—

No. He'd left marks on her wrist and burns from his smokes. That red light in the dark, like the devil's eye, never blinking, a harbinger of pain. She'd drifted from room to room with him, talking of Michelangelo, but he hadn't ever talked *with* her.

She scrabbled, feeling in a circle to ensure safe footing.

"Laura!"

His voice was so close. On her hands and knees now, she crawled, trembling, patting the ground in front of her before she moved ahead. Her fingers brushed a fissure in the rock.

Dangerous. Those caverns twisted for miles.

But she couldn't outrun him; he had that stupid flashlight. He would just find her again with a sweep of his arm.

She lowered herself into a crevice, legs dangling as if dropping into a pool, toeing for the bottom.

Light, blinding her. "Laura!"

She let go.

She fell, and fell and fell, away from the pearly string of streetlights that might have meant freedom.

Maybe I didn't die on Earth with Greg because hell is here. The devil wants his girl. Maybe I'm falling there now. I'm sorry —

Kesha's words echoed round in her mind. "You're responsible for you. Not for him."

She didn't want to say sorry again.

She stretched out her arms, trying to stay oriented as she fell, but her left knee s the side of the crevice and she tumbled, so maybe she was facing downwards, or sideways. The crevice narrowed and she braced against the rough surfaces with her hands and feet. Sharp little rocks tore up her palms as she slowed to a stop. She jammed her shoulder pretty bad, but that was better than the alternative.

A crunch of footsteps above. "Laura. I know that's you!"

He wouldn't follow her down here. Not into the crevice. The dark terrified him, like it scared most citizens of Fissure, because how would you know where to go if your flashlight ran out of energy? He carried the flashlight everywhere. Maybe he smoked just to keep another light source on him.

"Bitch! You know those things are like glaciers! They drop forever into lots of tunnels. You'll die in there!"

The light skittered around above her, to her right. She cringed away from it, and the curve and bend of the crevice hid her. She pushed against the sides, arms and legs trembling. The apology — automatic, trained — bubbled up her throat like vomit, pushed against her lips. She squashed her lips shut.

"You can try and find your way out, but you'll get lost! I can't believe you jumped in. I can't believe it, but I should've seen it. You were always so stupid —"

She tuned him out. She couldn't listen and focus on her muscles. *Hold on. Hold on. Don't make a sound. Stay out of the light.*

"I'm not responsible for him." She mouthed Kesha's words. "Just me. I have a responsibility for me."

He stayed for what seemed like hours, but could have been only minutes, or days. Her muscles complained that it lasted for centuries. But then the light, worming around nearby, flicked off. Footsteps crunched further away. Then the engine, revving in the distance.

With a sob, she dragged a foot towards where that light had gleamed and reached with one arm for a better hold. She hauled herself a few feet, muscles screaming, wet, bloody hands trying to grip.

After a few feet, she couldn't brace against the sides, and her damn hands! They kept slipping on the rocks.

She didn't know how far down she'd fallen, but she couldn't climb anymore. Before her mind could connect with the danger, she lowered herself deeper into the crevice, slow and steady, feeling for footholds in her converse. She wiped her bloody hands on her shirt — she needed them dry — but she couldn't stop and wrap them without something to balance her weight on.

Her shoulders and her forearms ached and threatened to give out. *Just one more time*, she told them. *Just let me find one more foothold.*

Then her grasping, shaking hands reached into a side space, a connecting fissure that wound horizontal. She clambered into it, letting her angry upper body rest. She tore her shirt and wrapped her bloody hands with the cloth, hoping the filthy fabric wouldn't give her an infection. Any layer of protection was better than gripping rocks and tearing her hands up more. She apologized to her hands, though, and that seemed right, saying sorry to herself instead of him.

The small connecting rift allowed her to wiggle inside. What if it tapered farther in, as the first one had? What if she couldn't back out? *They drop forever into lots of tunnels. You'll die in there!*

She shook his voice from her head.

The fissure snaked on and on, and she slept at some point, then continued. How long had she ducked and twisted through this crack? Had dawn peeked its head on the surface yet? Maybe Kesha had opened the diner already, wondering why Laura hadn't shown up for her shift.

Maybe she'd dreamed up this entire excursion to another planet. Maybe she'd never left Earth and was still living with Greg. Maybe she invented Ray to prove to herself nothing would change even if she tried. She persisted as the common denominator, right? She kept finding men like this. *You've always stuck yourself in a hole, in a chink of your subconscious, no way out, falling forever —*

No. No, she'd left his voice behind. She refused to return to it, to flutter around it, confused, like a butterfly around a sweet poison. She wasn't sorry. She walked a new path, and where it led, she did not know, except that it meant out.

Light.

It flooded the rift through a conjoining crevice. She recoiled, fearing his flashlight — no, fearing those smokes of his, burning, burning, shaming, punishing!

She blinked. The orange red of Fissure's sun shone down in a gentle warmth.

He couldn't rob the pleasure of light from her, not anymore.

The crevice remained narrow all the way up, so she could haul herself up easier, and the light showed her where to place her hands and feet. The cloth she'd wrapped around her bloody, sweaty palms allowed her to grip the protruding rocks without slipping. She made progress. Halfway there.

She didn't give her muscles a chance to falter. She dragged herself up with heaving breaths. Something tore in her shoulder, and she almost cried out, but that would waste her precious breath —

She made it to the top and collapsed on the ground. Allowed herself to cry.

She made space for the tears, now. She'd kept them locked in her throat so she wouldn't hope. She cried for herself, for what he had done to her. She cried for the desire now blooming in her chest for freedom and a future beyond him. She cried because she hadn't let herself before, and for the relief that now, she could.

The opening of the fissure lay in a crater, and the town waited close by, the first building maybe 300 yards off. The fissure had led her toward town like an underground, secret airlane.

But now, out in the open — in the sunrise — he could find her. Or one of his friends on the force might. *"Poor Mrs. Locke. Out alone all night, must've been drunk. Good thing nothing happened to her. Better take her right home."*

Her friend Kesha would fly the airlane soon for her shift at the diner. Laura gritted her teeth and jumped, landing halfway up the crater. She slid down a little, but clambered up and out, breathing heavily. The grimy, reddened cloth stuck to her hands, and she didn't unwrap it for fear of tearing more skin. She traipsed to the airlane roadside.

Sorry, she said to the streetlight. To Fissure's rising sun. *I wasn't afraid of you. I wasn't hiding from you.*

Kesha's old beater chugged along above her. Laura jumped up into the airlane and waved, and the sinking sensation made her laugh, because she'd decided to jump, to leave, to fall into a new life, aiming for the light.

She would not stay; she would not just come and go. She'd find a new place, a new life. Somewhere in the skies where she did not fear the light.

EMMIE CHRISTIE

Emmie Christie's (she/her) work tends to hover around the topics of feminism, mental health, cats, and the speculative such as unicorns and affordable healthcare. She has been published in Flash Fiction Online and in Three-Lobed Burning Eye and she graduated from the Odyssey Writing Workshop in 2013. She also enjoys narrating audiobooks for Audible. You can find her on her website, Twitter, Instagram, and Facebook.

Website: emmiechristie.com

Twitter & Instagram: @EmmieChristie33

Facebook: @EmmieChristieFiction

Whispered Navajo
BERNARDO VILLELA

There won't be room for them all in the double-wide, Doba thought. Despite that, the old Navajo man welcomed the group of twelve bedraggled folks into his home as his children and grandchildren stood guard around the perimeter.

He ran a mental headcount, beginning with three family units: a white mother and two kids, a Black man and his daughter, a Hispanic family of three. Also arriving was a tall, unaccompanied, white man, followed by two twenty-somethings — one wore a hijab, another a shaven-headed Korean-American woman. Bringing up the rear was a Black woman of indeterminate age that he pegged as a two-spirit.

Doba would ask for names out of politeness, but due to his age or as a defense mechanism many would slip his mind. Though the young lady in the hijab didn't speak, her name stayed with Doba: Parveen Farooqi.

"You can call me Doba," he told his guests. Doba motioned to the VW bus they had piled out of. "Best to swing it behind the trailer."

The white man, Roy — probably a nickname as he looked like Roy Rogers — went to move it.

"Amazed it still runs," Doba said when Roy returned.

Roy sighed. "Hasn't been easy."

With the vehicle secured, Doba asked everyone to turn out their pockets. Cash, no plastic; paper and pencils, no phones. Nothing to track them by. This was a well-rehearsed routine by now, but it never got less unnerving.

"Papers."

"The Pueblo didn't ask us for ID," the Caucasian mother, Lauren, said.

"Mom, don't be a Karen," her son said.

Doba smiled. "I haven't heard that one since I was young."

The Black man who introduced himself as Clarence was the first to offer his. Some in the group followed his lead, but others hesitated. Then the adults lined up, as they'd become accustomed to doing elsewhere, and showed Doba their identification papers. Lauren was the last holdout. She stayed back, clutching her bag tight, defending not only their contents, but herself.

"Even on the same rez, you'll find varying procedures. This is only so I can figure out if ICE might come by here," Doba insisted. Her fear was palpable. She had earned the right to distrust new people, but he wouldn't help her unless he knew the risks.

Lauren grumbled. It was as much resistance as she'd be allowed. Soon she was rummaging through her bag and handing over her papers.

Doba's grandson came in through the door, a bulky bag slung over his shoulder. "*Acheii*," Victor said, handing the satchel over to Doba. He looked through the mail delivery for the day to see if there was a matter more pressing than verifying the ID of these visitors, seeing there wasn't he tossed the satchel aside.

Looking around the room, Victor asked, "Refugees or outlaws?"

"Possibly both. We can feed them and keep them at least overnight."

Victor nodded and left to rejoin the Night-Guard.

Over the course of his life, Doba had become accustomed to welcoming outsiders onto the rez. In childhood, his instinct for who was or wasn't trustworthy was keen. As a young man, he had watched the borders with sweaty-palms and a loose grip on his shotgun, fearful the wrong kind of outsider would get in. His sense hadn't dulled. On occasion they'd encounter spies and informants friendly to the fascist regime who ruled the world beyond the rez, so now a leeriness lingered even after he decided someone was trustworthy.

Doba smelled deadwood burning. The law-keepers outside the rez built pyres along their borders to keep the undesirables out. The US government thought the pyres would also keep out those they deemed enemies of the state, making them easier to catch. The tribes speculated that the government saw the reservations as a means of exile for those fleeing US persecution.

For now, more respect was given to tribal sovereignty than to American citizens, but the Navajo tribes knew it was only a matter of time before the government stopped looking the other way, and the reservations ceased to be safe havens. Doba and the other tribal elders would always encourage those who sought refuge to move along as quickly as they could. *For everyone's safety.*

Doba reentered the double-wide and observed the group. Not only was this the largest number he had taken in, but this time, most were family units. It made him wonder how things were outside the rez. Too many people fleeing made him think his tribe could be in danger. Larger groups on the move implied coordination, and the feds thrived upon lording over a chaotic populace.

"Things are worse?" Doba asked the group.

"They didn't even have the decency to rewrite the Constitution, they just pissed on it," Roy grouched.

"I never put much stock in words on paper," Doba said, attempting to be genial. "As I told my grandson: After a day or two, for our safety, you should move on."

Nods and murmurs of assent circled the group of runaways. They were unwashed and looked as if they hadn't slept in days. The sunburn Lauren and her kids sported told Doba that they hadn't always all been piled in the VW Bus on their way here. Doba was sympathetic, but there was only so much he could do.

"We just need to regroup," Lauren said.

"We want to keep fighting back, but it's so difficult," Zora, the two-spirit Black woman, said.

"When the law becomes lawless, disorder is in order." Doba told them. Without waiting to see what they said in response, he went to see about getting them fed.

During the COVID pandemic, the Navajo, like many other tribes, became more isolated than they'd been before. As such, a return to consuming more traditional foods took hold. Lunch was generally a communal meal, so having guests join them for blue corn tortillas with kale, fry bread, and squash blossom soup was no hardship.

The guests gathered around a bonfire that illuminated the

falling twilight. Doba waited for the visitors to break the silence. He knew they'd have questions. Everyone did, if only to confirm their new normal wasn't normal at all.

"How often do people come through here?" Clarence asked.

"Folks like you? About once a month."

Clarence's daughter, Shawna picked at her fry bread. She hadn't eaten much, choosing to stick to her father's side by the fire. "Any other people?" she asked.

"Not since I was very young."

"Anyone ever stay for good?" Jackson asked. Doba interpreted it as a hopeful question, but the boy's voice was raspy and uncertain. The purple rings under his eyes were evidence of his transient existence, but unlike the other children, he held fast to hope despite his fatigue.

"One boy, very long ago . . ." Doba's eyes glazed, wandering back to the past. "But he had no family to go back to." Doba shook his head, remembering the small child approaching the gates, lost, alone, grieving. He had come to the rez over thirty years ago. "You have families. He was running from social workers," he concluded, shaking his head to try to get that bittersweet memory of a difficult but still better time out of his mind.

"If the feds don't come here, why do we have to leave?" Jackson asked. Lauren swatted his hand.

"It's a fair question, Lauren, is it?" Doba said with a smile. He sipped some tea. "Not unlike something the boy who stayed would ask." Doba paused to gather his thoughts and took his sweet time answering. "The difference is that now, they're having trouble holding people down."

Jackson opened his mouth as if to speak. Lauren put her hand on his, and Jackson seemed to decide against it.

"Not that the feds have lost control," Doba continued. "But they have to work very hard to maintain power."

"Based on what?" Kyan, the Korean-American girl, asked.

"Do you come from big cities?" Doba asked. Nearly all of them nodded their heads. Doba continued, "Are people on the streets? Risking arrest? Do the authorities flex to prove it's a police state? Call in reinforcements?"

They sat in awestruck silence broken only by the hooting of an owl in the distance.

"I'm not a vision, not a naked Indian."

"*Shizhé'é*, they're not old enough to know *The Doors*." Doba's eldest son, Thomas, laughed.

"Speak for yourself," Zora said.

"The tribal police, here and elsewhere, are in a precarious place," Doba clarified.

"So it's true?" Roy asked.

"What's true?" Jackson asked Roy.

Roy ignored Miguel and repeated the question.

That was not lost on Doba. His manner of speaking was deliberate regardless, but Doba slowed a bit more now, to read them. "A lot of times we end up — our cops end up — as double-agents. When protests flared in Phoenix and Santa Fe, local and federal authorities requested our back up. Ain't that a hoot? When we've agreed, the feds agreed to step back, but some tribal policemen do assist the Resistance. In other places, the tribal police disbanded, figuring if there was no police force no one would try to go there."

"Have you spoken to those reservations? Do they feel safer?" Roy asked.

Loaded question, Doba thought. He wanted to put them at ease, but he couldn't. Doba shrugged. "So far."

Hearing this, Zora, Parveen, and some of the adults exchanged a knowing look.

As conversation around the bonfire died down, Victor

nodded to Doba to indicate he was going to round up his crew for the Night-Guard.

After all the guests had settled for the night, Doba sat in his double-wide watching the patrols. There wasn't a sound in the darkness except for the occasional stirrings from the Night-Guard, but Doba didn't tire. He never slept much when they had visitors.

The following morning, Doba instructed his family to leave the sleeping bags out as the visitors might need more rest. The visitors didn't take Doba up on that offer, which made Doba sit in pensive observation until he had to start his own day, regardless of his guests. The day burned into night without incident. Despite this, Doba was on edge. He recited some of "Walking in Beauty" under his breath: *Hózhó náhásdlíí'*. But he didn't feel the negative depart him, nor that things would become beautiful again.

Something was coming, he knew it. He felt it the same way his old bone fractures told him rain was coming.

NOREEN WOODHOUSE CAME to Arizona with her husband for her health. The dry air would make her golden years more comfortable, soothe her respiratory ills. They lucked out finding this house just outside the Navajo rez. They were isolated. It was perfect. She was tired of life in the big city. The constant chanting, clashing of police and protestors grated her nerves. Little did she know that living near the rez would get under her skin too.

They had seen the VW bus rumble down the old dirt road. "Forget the bus," Harold had said.

She couldn't. Noreen stared down the road for a few

minutes after the van disappeared from sight. "Why would anyone drive that rust-bucket unless —"

"It's only the rez that way. It's probably just a family lost on the way to the Grand Canyon. We'll probably see them heading the other way soon."

They didn't.

Noreen continued raising the topic. Harold asked her to leave it alone with less and less patience, like a mother nagging a child to leave a scab alone. Still, Noreen couldn't let it go. She'd seen more than one vehicle trudge down that road and never return.

"Where else could it have gone?"

"They could've righted their course without passing this way." Harold harrumphed. She pretended like she'd really given up the notion to Harold and stewed on it. She knew the feds liked to leave Antifa to rot on the rez . . . but what if this was different?

What if the police or FBI came and asked if you saw a VW bus drive by heading toward the Navajo. You're a bad liar. You saw their plates, Noreen! You noticed flaked paint over the left taillight! They'll know you saw. Then you'll end up in lady-jail. A bull-dyke's bitch.

Later, when Harold lay zonked out on the couch watching the Diamondbacks play, Noreen called 911.

As the sun sank below the horizon, Agent Glenallen arrived for his graveyard shift at Homeland Security's HQ. He expected to catch up on paperwork and half-listen to the Diamondbacks get walloped in the night game of a double-header.

The order to pursue the Navajo Reservation lead surprised

him. Those suspected of being on the VW bus were wanted for sedition, but so were a lot of people. It was the catchall charge nowadays. Glenallen didn't think the call warranted a response. Parveen Farooqi may've still been in that VW Bus with a large group, but they were on a rez, not causing any trouble. The dangerous dissidents were fleeing into Sonora and Baja. He'd rather stop people at the checkpoints. Insubordination would land him in a Dissident Camp though. He grumbled under his breath, put on his aviators, and mobilized his men.

Parveen sat on a squat bench outside the double-wide, observing the sun coloring the sky with swaths of red and orange. Her traveling companions slept inside, their sleeping-bag-covered bodies creating a tiny mountain range. In a previous life, she loved taking long weekend drives to places like Monument Valley and Crested Butte to paint landscapes. It was cheaper than therapy.

Parveen's eyes stung from memories of bygone times. Times when the news would anger her to political artwork, not the frontlines of demonstrations. She had tried watching the sun-painting develop, but the zephyrs that came that nightfall back blew dirt and tumbleweeds about, forcing Parveen to shield her face in her hijab. As always, her garb only instigated the wind as it did passersby on the street who couldn't just let people be.

Doba walked out holding a glass. "Water?" he asked.

Parveen accepted. "Why are you still up?" she asked.

"A bad feeling."

The door to the double-wide across the way banged open.

"*Yíkai!*" Thomas shouted, a terror laced through his voice. Doba's bad feeling had come to fruition.

Parveen's eyes immediately focused on the gate. Crosshatched shafts of light glared through the chain link fence. Gasping, she stood and entered Doba's double-wide to wake everyone up.

Doba looked on at the common but unsettling sight: federal vehicles approaching the rez. He projected calm to the young men in the guard towers, his grandsons among them. Itchy trigger-fingers were the last thing he needed. A tall white man stepped out of the car, removed his hat, and put on aviator sunglasses. Doba had no respect for men who shielded their eyes. Aviator Glass's subordinates exited the vehicle. None brandishing a weapon. *Yet.*

"Let me in," the federal officer growled to Doba.

"What's your business?" Doba asked as he approached the gate seeking to minimize the disturbance.

"You know I don't have to ask. I was being courteous."

Doba huffed. "You *didn't* ask."

"We're looking for a fugitive."

Doba remained stone-faced, coaxing the man in the aviators to state what he knew. Aviator Glasses recited his dossier. Doba sighed. "Why you think they stopped instead of passing through?" Doba often mangled his grammar in dealings with Feds so he'd be underestimated.

"That's my business. Will you let me in?"

Doba glanced up at his two sons. They stood at attention awaiting a command. His teaching them the positions of the white military saddened him, but it was a safety mechanism. "Open the gates, boys."

Doba was relieved the Feds had not assumed the dissidents were being harbored. If Aviator Glasses thought foul play was involved, he'd not have been so kind.

Doba stepped aside. Victor climbed down the observation deck and opened the gate. Doba took a breath to remain calm. He knew that their unwillingness to enter uninvited would change someday, but he kept to the decision his father had made: the path of least resistance should be chosen until the *Diné* were provoked. Even after the Navajo Wars, The Long Walk, reservation life, and COVID had ravaged his people, Doba still believed that the Holy People would help his clan. It was this thought — *and only this thought* — that kept him calm as Aviator Glasses and his men entered his home.

These men were more militarized than Doba remembered. He was unsure how wide a net they'd cast on the rez, but he was not going to restrict them. Doba eased their entry at each dwelling they decided to enter. The less resistance he displayed, the less thoroughly they'd search, and the sooner they'd be on their way, or so he hoped. Yet when Aviator Glasses and his men searched around the other double-wides and came up empty, they decided they wanted to look in Doba's place.

HAVING SERVED the purpose of making him seem disconnected, Glenallen tucked the aviators into his breast pocket. As he searched trailers, kitchenettes, water closets, beds, and so on, he shuffled through his mental index of outlaws.

Lauren Norris: Distribution of Propaganda. Translation:

handing out flyers, low-tech organization of the Resistance. Rarely at protests, she shielded her kids until authorities connected her to specific events. She bolted; an annoyance, not a threat. The person printing the fliers was a far more desirable catch.

On a table, Glenallen saw a cup of tea and a glass of water. Glenallen was poised to ask whose water it was, when Thomas entered, grabbed the glass and drank some.

In the kitchenette, opening bland cabinets made from fabricated wood, Glenallen pondered Clarence Brown: a lawyer who, upon offering pro bono services to Black Lives Matter protesters, was charged with material support for terrorist acts. That put him on the run.

Benito and Paloma Carvajal came to mind as Glenallen looked under the sink and in drawers for any evidence of houseguests in hiding.

Parveen Farooqi, disruptive in Patriotic Education classes: Refused to recite the Pledge, knelt during the anthem, refused compulsory prayer, but proved the curriculum's success, she didn't convince anyone to join her. After schooling, she found the Resistance. Her convictions were strong but she wasn't a leader. Neither a danger, nor a lone wolf. Locating her could lead them to many little bosses within the Resistance.

Glenallen opened a pantry closet. It was full of shotguns. "What's this?"

"You know what those are," Doba said from behind him.

"Got paperwork for these?"

Doba glared at Glenallen. "You came looking for a fugitive —"

"If you're harboring them —"

"They certainly wouldn't give up their arms."

The guns had caught Glenallen off-guard, but he was glad to have angered the old Navajo. The artillery also gave

Glenallen the hope of catching Roy Williamson, the only man suspected of being on the VW bus approaching the rez. Williamson had wounded officers defending so-called protestors, and had procured illegal firearms for the Resistance. Glenallen wanted to collar him, but having him on the run was better than having him in the thick of things.

Glenallen exited the trailer. A very concerned Doba followed.

Glenallen circled the double-wide as the other man stood watch. He had thought he saw the VW bus there, but when he rounded the corner, there was nothing. The bus must have been moved.

Glenallen huffed, then hollered to his men. They would go down the driveway and toward the arroyos and mesas. One look back at Doba revealed anxiety on the old man's face.

Yet by the end of the night, no VW bug was to be found. Glenallen would return. Something was there. Glenallen knew fear when he saw it.

DOBA CAME out to see Victor and the other Night-Guards at the southeast entrance to the rez. Looking into the dark shadows and moonlight-colored expanse beyond the road, Doba noticed the DHS unit approaching the arroyo that cut through a trio of mesas Doba called the Three Bears. They sped down the dirt road, high beams glaring at the Doba and Raven, a young Night Guard.

Speaking in whispered Navajo, Raven asked, "Isn't that where our visitors are?"

Doba signaled for quiet.

The federal vehicles screeched to a halt atop the arroyo.

The agents came out of their cars, weapons at the ready. In unison they approached the rocky outcropping, flashlights held above their firearms.

"THIS IS THE DEPARTMENT OF HOMELAND SECURITY!" an unseen bullhorn announced.

Doba and Raven didn't move from their spot, but across the rocky landscape, Doba saw Parveen climb out from behind a rocky outcropping and walk out into the arroyo, hands raised.

Roy lay atop the middle mesa of the Three Bears, gripping his shotgun. "What the hell is she doing?" Roy whispered when he saw Parveen step out from her hiding spot.

Clarence grumbled as he lay next to him. "Sacrificing herself for the greater good."

"They're not here to make an arrest," Roy growled back, nearly losing control of his voice. Roy was angry. He knew resisting a fascistic government was about more than just one life, but why had they come up here if not to shower them with bullets?

On the far mesa, Raven and Victor watched Parveen approach the Feds above her as if watching a play. Even at this distance, they could clearly see the agents under Glenallen's command training their weapons on Parveen. Glenallen just stood in complete stillness. Waiting.

Raven took out her cellphone and hit record.

GLENALLEN STOOD in front of his men with his fist raised. He watched Parveen and her surroundings carefully. He was wary of a trap, but he didn't want to make a martyr of her.

The woman walked slowly towards him. Glenallen wanted to sigh in relief. This was going to be a quick arrest. It would be worth all the paperwork he would have to do.

Then, someone to his left opened fire.

Glenallen unleashed a stream of expletives he couldn't hear over the barrage of bullets.

PALOMA THOUGHT her silence was her best quality. She would not speak unless it was necessary. Now her voice was needed. The kids were behind Roy and Clarence, but she needed to make sure they all laid down flat, including her son Miguel.

"Headshots only!" Roy instructed his snipers through gritted teeth. Their shots would give away their position, so they needed as many kills as possible before a return of fire. The quickest victory was the surest one.

Roy and his group had come to the rez to avoid a fight. The feds had brought it anyway.

"WHO DID IT? DID I SAY FIRE?" Glenallen screamed. As his bellowed question echoed, a round of gunfire rained down upon them from the mesa-top above.

Turning, Glenallen spotted muzzle-flare, a constellation of earthbound stars, atop the mesa. A hot wind buzzed by him. Glenallen froze as a second round came their way. He raised his firearm before realizing five of his men were down, at least one looked dead. Glenallen and the two remaining men returned fire as they were showered with a third hail of bullets. With a quick side-eyed glance, he saw it was the morons who started the firefight who remained standing. *Of course they would still be alive*, Glenallen thought, cursing the fates.

Another barrage of bullets assaulted them. The two men were knocked back, their return-fire going wild. As they stumbled back, twin spouts of blood burst forth from their necks.

ON THE MESA, Roy lay on his back, a smile still on his face from seeing his team bring down the Feds. He stood, taking a lingering glance down into the arroyo. His eyes met those of the lone man below. And his rifle. Moments later, Roy hit the ground. Across the way, Roy eyed Clarence, doubled over, his shirt crimson. Zora stood over him, firing into the arroyo below.

DOBA OPENED his pantry and grabbed a shotgun.

"*Shizhé'é ha'át'íí baa naniná?*" Victor asked Doba.

"I'm ending this."

Doba stepped onto his porch. The star-strewn sky left him feeling melancholy. If the Holy People didn't intervene, there was not a person on the continent who cared about their fate. With his son and grandsons by his side, Doba shuffled in silence toward the arroyo, shotguns aimed at the federal agents.

Their breaths fell into sync. Inhale, exhale. Then a zephyr came from behind Doba, embraced him, and caressed his trigger finger.

Together, they fired.

IT RAINED blood and gray matter. In the confluence of gunfire, Glenallen and his last two foot-soldiers were hit first by Zora's shots and then again by those fired by three generations of Navajo on behalf of countless generations of all tribes. Under the rocky gaze of the Three Bears, Glenallen, Orman, and Unger fell aground lifeless. There they would lay until the sun intensified their putrefaction and the vultures came to feast.

When the smoke settled, the Resisters collected their dead. Lauren came out from hiding in the van and said an unceremonious farewell to Doba before quietly rounding up the survivors.

LATER THAT NIGHT, Raven watched the video. She didn't realize she provided commentary under her breath in Navajo. She subtitled the video and uploaded it to the Internet hoping to speak not only to the Resistance, but to affect the third of the population who still supported this regime and the other third who were apathetic.

The visitors who survived the battle left without hesitation, it was expected, yet Zora, Lauren, and Paloma all wrote later—in letters that made it to the rez's hand-delivery system —to express their condolences for the trouble they brought and the hurry with which they vanished. Raven, now married to Victor and about to celebrate a Blessingway with her son Ashkii, responded simply to that apology with a line from a Navajo prayer:

"*Hózhó náhásdlíí'.*"

BERNARDO VILLELA

Bernardo Villela has short fiction included in periodicals such as *Coffin Bell Journal*, *The Dark Corner Zine*, *Constraint 280* and forthcoming in *Rivet*. He's had stories included in anthologies such as *101 Proof Horror, A Monster Told Me Bedtime Stories, From the Yonder II,* and *Disturbed*. He has had poetry published by *Entropy*, *Zoetic Press*, and *Bluepepper* and others. You can find Bernardo on his website, Twitter, and Instagram.

Website: miller-villela.com

Twitter: @BernardoVillela

Instagram: @bernardodeassisvillela

HELL OF A MIND, HEAVEN OF A MIND
RASHMI AGRAWAL

F*ifty-one hours to the murder*
   I convulse in fear at the thought. It's been ages since I've killed anyone. I'm out of practice. Heck, I'm out of choices, too.

And I failed to inform the school about my absence. They hate finding a substitute teacher last minute.

I drop my phone on the empty nightstand and pull the quilt up to my forehead. The darkness beneath the cover envelops me. It bites sharper than the snow outside. Once the oxygen reduces inside the quilt, I uncover my face and breathe fast, as if the air within the walls of my shanty is the last ounce of oxygen and someone might suck it away from me.

What is abundant here, anyway?

Whirr... whirr...

Before I can inhale to my heart's content, the phone vibrates again. The tilted side table, its one leg resting on a stack of unstable bricks, wobbles. Or so it feels. Everything is trembling after Sharad's morning call. *How did he find my daughter's location?*

I snatch the phone and glare at the screen. Another private number. I have no choice but to answer.

"Robin! It's me again." That voice, that same heavy tenor that I never want to hear again, says, ". . . that shit . . . not worth . . . is valuable." Many of his words escape my ears as my brain refuses to register them.

I reply inanimately, and those words soon fall from my mind as well.

"How have you been?" Sharad's voice rings fake. He's coercing me to do his dirty work again. How wrong I was to think he'd never find me, reach me, force me again. Because of the sudden upheaval he has caused in my aloof, low-key life, I feel dizzy. The food in my stomach lurches up. I try to withhold the inflection of emotions in my voice.

We discuss: I talk and question; Sharad answers. He elaborates his plan for the assault I have to make. Then he talks about Charmi's wellbeing. A threatening innuendo hammers my brain. He must have fished out my location too. The kind of place I live in is not on the atlas. Heck, perhaps not even on Google Maps.

Sharad yet again instructs me to eliminate someone for him. On my denial, he reminds me of his favors. *Nasty old favors.* His plea is a demand. Keeping the stammer in check, I deny again. So, he talks about Charmi once more, his tone resembling a warning rather than a conversation now. *Damn! Oh, Charmi, my darling!* I surrender for her sake and reluctantly agree to assassinate a stranger despite fleeing Sharad's homicidal business years ago.

My thoughts are so focused on my daughter's safety that I don't realize Sharad has disconnected the line. I toss the phone on the bed and hide under the tattered quilt again, feeling sick.

Sharad hinted that he would deploy Charmi into prostitution if I ditch him or run away this time. It's easy for him: the trafficking, ransoms, the killing. But Charmi is still a child. *My child.* So what if I'm not her biological father? I had promised her safety to my dying wife. I would rather die than fail them.

Sharad has always been determined to achieve big, to accomplish his desires. Success has an altered definition for him; I once followed the same glossary. In the disguise of a naïve-looking physics teacher, Sharad lurks among us; the persona he hides from the world is soaked in people's blood.

I clutch the bedsheet under me. Morsels of food try to purge their way out of my stomach again.

How can I ever forget the day Sharad first approached me with his plans to make money? I was easy bait — a money-deprived math teacher and an outcast from society. I didn't realize he intended me to be his executioner. I was cajoled by this physics geek and his comrade, Lala, who was a technology menace. His amazing device —

Ring —

My antique phone beeps once then dies. I need time to settle my rampant heartbeats. A craving arises. A warm bottle of alcohol will relieve my tension.

I skitter down to Wang's Daily, a food store on the opposite side of the road. Wangmo doesn't like to lend items to her customers. And I must ask for a credit today. Brandy costs more than the few coins I have. Not that I borrow there often.

As I walk into the store, Wangmo is having a war of words with a customer. Her cashier stands by looking confused. Not a golden time to ask her for a tiny debt. I find a bottle, which isn't brandy but should calm my jitters. When I urge Wangmo to let me have the liquor on loan, she pauses, averts her focus from her victim, and rolls her eyes at me. I stare at the old gibbering mound of selfishness. Wangmo focuses back on her acrimonious row with the customer, her arms moving in the air again and spittle flying out of her mouth.

A perfect opportunity to test my dormant skill in preparation for the task ahead!

I focus on Wangmo's face and squint. Everything around her fades into the background. Her hands stop moving; she stills, her mouth agape. She stands silent, staring at me. Her victim softly sneaks out of the store. Wangmo doesn't budge an inch. *Looks like her brain waves are under my grasp now.* Upon my silent signal, she nods blankly and presses a green button to disable the security alarm at the exit. The employee at the cash counter objects, but I keep my control on the woman. Wangmo nods at the cashier, and he waives my payment.

Thank God! At least the device Sharad implanted inside my head still works.

I rush toward the exit, bottle in hand, not believing my success, though a mild ache pinches my skull. I clutch my forehead. As my focus wanes, my grasp on Wangmo shatters. I bolt through the doorway, ignoring her incessant shouts behind me, but happy that time hasn't dampened the device's controlling power.

49 HOURS *to the murder*

I gulp large sips from the bottle. The intense, warm flavor touches every nerve of my brain. People swear by *Ara's* strength and taste. It's one of the best local liquors. The flavor is not new to me — a favorite from college days. Slowly, *Ara* kicks out the tension. Is this calmness triggered by the unanticipated victory of the device, the one Sharad's assistant Lala installed?

Lala — an expelled scientist from a government-based research organization in India — devised the brainwaves manipulator B-Waer. They cajoled me into a trap. I was easily swept. The money they offered was more than enough to fulfill the dreams of my wife, Dohna. My teacher's salary would never have provided for our own home and future children.

Initially, their ploy was limited to activities that made easy bucks. I was blinded by the financial rewards.

It took me days of practice on one of Sharad's puppets, resulting in a perpetual headache. My first assignment was to play with the brainwaves of a business tycoon. The conspiracy against the rich man went on for three days as I slowly instructed him to ruin his business. Without a clue of being controlled, the man auctioned off all his stakes and assets then transferred the property to his younger brother.

They then forced me to do the unspeakable with the lure of more money. In fear, I acquiesced. The ruined man divorced his gorgeous wife and killed his accountant. *That poor man!* All so that his brother could inherit the business and betroth the tycoon's wife.

A few days later, Sharad's destitute puppet went missing, never to be found again. As Sharad and Lala celebrated their success, more projects rolled in. Soon, he was neck-deep in the contract-killing business, still camouflaging as a physics teacher. With B-Waer, success had become easier and my yearning to earn money for Dohna became his opportunity. His business thrived, my humanity died. As did so many people.

Charmi's giggles flood my mind and pull me from my regret. *Ara* has shown its effect. I feel numb and light on my feet. I need more practice; I scan't bungle the task like I did six years ago. My thoughts settle on Wangmo. She comes as easy prey. I close my eyes and envisage her wrinkled face, shouting at her store's cashier last week, spit flying and hands waving up and down, all in slow motion.

My left eye wavers, and I struggle against the crushing fatigue; my dysfunctional glass eye never revolts. I try to visualize today's encounter. The fresher the memory, the better should be my control. But today's scene doesn't fill the space beyond my closed eyes. All I see is a little girl dribbling a brown ball — my Charmi.

Charmi dribbles the ball and passes it; Dohna misses it. Charmi says something inaudible, twisting her lips into a frown, and Dohna runs toward our daughter and pulls her into an embrace.

The phone jingles in the background, but I remain indifferent. I enjoy seeing my girls laughing and playing. Slowly, I zone out, and the darkness closes in.

33 HOURS to the murder

"Please don't mess this up, Robin." Sharad's voice has a hint of hesitation today.

"Dammit, the last project was . . ." I clench my teeth. "I lost my Dohna that time, and Charmi became an orphan again. I haven't seen my daughter in years."

"Fuck, Robin, that was your own glitch." Sharad lets out a sigh, his voice mellow when he speaks again. "Look, buddy, I'm sorry for what happened."

Is he really, though?

"Just this once, OK? I won't trouble you again, Robin."

"One last time. For my daughter. After this, don't contact me ever. Did you get me?" I bang my mobile on the three-legged table.

I'm not running away like I did the last time. This new courage feels liberating. In a few more months, Charmi's schooling will end. I can take Charmi with me and dissolve into anonymity, away from Sharad's prying eyes. Bhutan has many tiny pockets of towns to hide the two of us. I won't leave Charmi in someone's care. Before Dohna and I adopted her, she lived many years miserable and in near-orphan status with her intemperate single father. *Still doing so, my poor child.*

But will Sharad really stop pestering me after this? He managed to find me here and he can find us later. Running away from him would be futile. This must be the last time.

AFTER I HAD COMPLETED several successful executions, Sharad had wanted to insert B-Waer into his own skull. Success had made him greedier and unhappier. Removing the device from my brain could have killed me. So, Lala designed another B-Waer for Sharad while I continued to manipulate Sharad's prey at his behest.

Lala had also fitted a small device called Shield inside Sharad's head that could mask his thoughts from me, but destiny had a different plan for us. Lala passed away of a heart attack before he could install the better version of the untested new B-Waer inside Sharad's head. I wonder what became of the other device.

Just the thought of him having access to such technology is frightening. Maybe he already has Charmi. I decide to call my daughter.

I struggle with my mobile as the mild headache returns like the nonstop echo of a faraway drill machine. A side effect of resurrecting the device. When I dial Charmi's hostel's number, it goes unanswered. I should call her more often, but the fear for her safety always subdues my desire to be in touch. So, I keep our conversations occasional. Short, and crisp. And I've never shared my number with her. But what purpose has this safety served? She's traced; I'm tracked. We both are vulnerable now. I dial her mobile; it's not reachable. I decide to call her again later that night.

Before that, I need to be ready for my last mission.

After locking the front door, I slip the key into my *gho's* pouch and scamper toward my target. Being the middle of a working day, the road is uncrowded. I pause outside Wang's Daily, peer through the glass door, and narrow my eyes. Wangmo's body comes to a standstill, and her hands freeze midair. *Ah, smooth!*

I plant my idea in Wangmo's mind, and her slap echoes within the store, leaving a young man caressing his cheek. I had a row with him many weeks ago. Revenge taken. The man opens the store's door with full force. It swings toward me and slams my nose. My already aching head spins, and I whither in pain. My vision blurs. A constellation of black stars fills the vision in my good eye. I squat right there on the sidewalk; a few red drops trickle on the thin layer of snow. The blood is thick inside my nose. I glance inside the shop window and see Wangmo blink, gaze pointed in my direction. I feel like a criminal caught red-handed.

Wangmo's staring continues. The control is still active, thankfully, so I demand from her one more service: a bottle. Cupping my face, I dash back toward my shanty. I release my mental grip on her by focusing on the beautiful memories of my dismantled family, the bottle clutched in my fist.

20 HOURS to the murder

I've traveled ten hours for this stupidity. To look at my victim and create her memories for tomorrow. My victim will read her controversial book snippets and discuss her liberating feminist and political ideas before walking to her death. Anger boils up, but I stuff it down and think of Charmi. I have a job to do. *For Charmi.*

I wait outside the airport in the biting cold and thick darkness next to the man carrying the author's placard. I feel downright stupid as I've no guest to attend to, so I dial Charmi's number. Charmi is still not reachable. *Where's she right now?*

I catch a glimpse of my target for a good three minutes when she comes out and boards the cab. Her brain frequency is very noisy, as if multiple things are competing for dominance in her mind. Quite common with famous folks.

That was the case six years back when that famous neurosurgeon refused to operate on my boss to implant the new B-Waer. I had been ordered to follow the doctor as he was playing and roaming with his son in a shopping mall in Mumbai. My gaze diverted to the love of my life, who was in the crowd, too. Dohna's smiling face cemented in my consciousness, and I lost control on the neurosurgeon's brainwaves.

Instead of the neurologist, it was Dohna who jumped over the railing on the seventh floor. Standing at the edge, clutching at a shopping bag, young Charmi screamed as her foster mother fell to her death. The neurosurgeon was left unscathed, but my life burned thread by thread as Dohna's life succumbed to my cruel manipulations.

Gradually, the silicon demon dwelling inside my skull clouded my right eye. I couldn't function. I was drowning in guilt and regret. Sharad wasn't ready to compromise his business for my health. So, I ran away before I could botch another job, and poor Charmi was once again an orphan. I entrusted her to a teacher I knew from my childhood at a small boarding school in the sleepy eastern hills of Arunachal Pradesh and fled to Bhutan, my birth land. The small village became my safe haven.

It has been six years now.

When Charmi's number is still not reachable, I call her hostel warden. She mentions a trip. My heart screams in fear when the warden mentions that Charmi's trip approval form was signed and paid in full.

What trip? Who sponsored it?

I need to find Charmi. Did Sharad hurt my child already?

The principal of the school where I teach calls for the third time. My two days' absence must have panicked him. I conveniently ignore him. People do fall sick occasionally, take uninformed leaves, and don't pick calls, too.

When the mobile rings for the fourth time, I reply, "I'm ill; I'll be in the day after tomorrow, Mr. Jigme."

Familiar laughter roars on the other end of the line. Sharad, not the principal. Damn, more than his impatience, his laughter irritates me.

"Where is my daughter? What the hell did you —"

"Fuck, man, I've no idea what you are talking about. I should've kidnapped her. Would have saved myself from your gibber all this time; it would have been easier this way." His laughter stabs my ear. When I don't retaliate, he calms down. "OK. I'll tell you after this assignment."

I tighten my fist; his words are like molten iron pouring into my ears.

"Just one more day," he adds. *Just one more day.* "You will receive a ticket for the venue," saying curtly, before hanging up.

12 HOURS to the murder

There's an orange envelope stuck inside the doorjamb in my ramshackle lodging room. It's six in the morning, and the sunlight has yet to touch the city. My phone beeps. *Jogger's Trails*, the text from Sharad reads.

I sit on the floor against the door — a pass for the event and my mobile in hand — and think about Charmi. Feeling uneasy, I rest my head on my knees. A knot twists in my gut. I rush to the bathroom, but can't even cross the seven feet between the two doors. After Dohna's death, I've never been so nervous.

Charmi's giggles fill my mind. I shouldn't have left her at the hostel. She would have been safer here with me. But I can't turn the wheel of time. I must get ready for this last felony for my daughter's sake.

I get up and rush to the park to follow my victim and catch a glimpse of her one final time before the act.

1 HOUR to the murder

A group of guards surrounds the entrance to the auditorium. *I'm not an intruder, I've got a ticket,* I reassure myself for the umpteenth time.

Why would anyone want to kill a writer for her controversial bestselling book? This is weird; Sharad never took such contracts, but money is a bitch, isn't it? And Sharad is a lustful dog, always hungry, salivating at every opportunity and slurping it down without a second thought.

I pull out the phone and reject the hungry dog's incoming call.

When I enter the auditorium, the crowd is settling down. The program is about to begin. I find my target and concentrate on her face. The writer's skin is sagging, eyes rimmed with purple circles, but lips smiling. She looks simple but somehow classy, too. Like a composed intellectual.

The author flinches and sinks deep into her seat on the stage as a host takes his place at the dais. A giant chandelier hanging overhead illuminates their faces. I find a seat in the second row. The closer the distance, the better I can work.

A hand touches my shoulder. I shudder at the unwanted pressure. Not wanting any distraction, I tell the person behind me to get off. The hand remains, so I grip the wrist and move it away without looking back. They murmur something.

Damn, it's him. My confidence immediately falters.

I start my game as Sharad whispers a warning in my ear. The writer is saying my words now, a script I was given with the ticket. She coughs and clears her throat, perhaps realizing that she isn't speaking in favor of her book. People hoot at her.

She becomes flustered. Her voice falters as if trying to fight back. She squirms in her seat, eyes wide. I try harder. The author expresses a desire to kill a political leader in anger. The host asks her to calm down and read the first chapter of her book.

She complies. Once she finishes reading, the host calls upon the winner of some contest for whom they have arranged a Bhutan tour.

The young girl climbing the stairs appears familiar with her black ringlets of hair and calm gait. *Wait, is that...?*

It's my Charmi! She's a beautiful adolescent now. I've seen

her virtually only on her birthdays. She looks so lovely in real life. But why is she *here*?

I crane my neck. The seat behind me is empty.

My Charmi walks on stage and is talking to the writer. My vision floods with images of Charmi's face. Memories from her childhood fill my mind. Charmi glances my way, an odd expression on her face. If I manipulate any brain wave, it might be Charmi's. I can't risk her life. I try to shrug off the glimpses and concentrate on the writer's face. A sharp jolt hammers my head from within. I clutch my face, withering in pain. The device is confused between the targets.

Charmi pushes the famous novelist to the ground. Her bodyguard straightens his rifle at my daughter.

Heck, this can't be happening!

I direct all my power at Charmi to command her to apologize, but she's cemented in place. The writer beckons the bodyguard to lower his rifle. The audience gasps as she slaps Charmi. My heart sinks.

Charmi is frozen on her spot on the stage. The kid has a history of physical abuse at the hands of her father before coming to the orphanage where Dohna worked. So much can go wrong. I must do something! Through the pain, I push harder on Charmi's mind.

My daughter does not move. Why is Charmi not moving? Why is my device failing me?

I look around and catch the semblance of the cruel man hiding behind the dais. Sharad seems to be focused on the two women as if . . . as if . . . *Oh no, no, no! Fuck no.* I run towards him, but balk when I see what's happening on the stage.

Charmi has a rifle pointing at the bodyguard who is holding his stomach, cringing in pain on the stage. One of her feet has pinned him down. The author hides behind her chair.

People behind me start murmuring and scattering around

the room. Charmi points the rifle at the crowd. Her eyes are full of fear. The commotion in the back increases, loaded with screams and chaotic movements. *Damn, I must stop her from pressing the trigger.* People bolt towards the exit gate, causing a tiny stampede, a handful duck behind the chairs, and a few folks stand amused at the exhibition onstage.

I pull up all my splendid memories of Charmi: her playing on my lap, riding on my back, eating ice creams furtively from the fridge, her charming face from her birthday calls in the hostel. These memories are so vivid that I relive all the moments with her from our past as if I've actually turned the wheel of time. I can feel my brain waves touching Charmi's now, but her thoughts are noisy, deflecting away from my control. I demand her to drop the rifle, but she doesn't budge an inch.

Sharad . . . he's controlling her. Or both the women? *Oh God, he has gotten the second B-Waer fitted.* Lala had mentioned that the new B-Waer could control more than one person at a time. I won't let him use my daughter. *I won't.* I concentrate on Charmi again, but her brain waves won't budge. They are beyond my control.

I step closer to the stage and call her name with conviction. And as if telepathy has connected us, she looks up. Our gazes meet. Her eyes go wide, and she jumps several steps back, away from the bodyguard. She chucks the rifle away from herself, the author, and the guard.

The author jumps at Charmi. I reach for the author's brain frequencies, ask her to stay put. The author stops her assault and calms, now standing confused. Charmi pounces on her. *I have to stop them from hurting each other.* No one will ever care for a teenager's pleas when a famous author's safety is compromised.

I must stop Sharad from controlling them. I jump and push

the dais at him. The stage groans and heaves, jostling Sharad from his stance behind it. Sharad tumbles backwards. The two women fall to their knees. This might have broken his grasp and give me enough time for the next step.

In my mind, I call upon my daughter to remember Dohna. I ask Charmi to take the writer away from the scene, away from Sharad, but she resists. Before Sharad can regain control of the author, I reach for Charmi's brainwaves one last time and insist she leave with the author.

After three grueling seconds, I see them exit the back door.

The cruel offender gets up from behind the dais. I cross Sharad's brainwaves — violent and purporting. Is the Shield malfunctioning or dysfunctional?

His B-Waer bisects mine, launching his negative judgments inside my head. I rush the stage and pick up the rifle Charmi left behind. I stand to see a small fleet of guards marching in with their weapons pointing at us. When an urge kicks in to kill everyone around me, I recall the last good time with my family. Sharad's control on me weakens, and my murderous desire wanes.

I turn the rifle to the floor. "Why Charmi?" I ask Sharad.

He crackles with cachinnation. "Your daughter knows my secrets. Yours too."

"But you also have the B-Waer. Why trouble me?"

"All in the fucking game, buddy. It is fun to get a daughter killed by her father. And you deserve a punishment for ditching me last time." His monstrous laughter burdens the already heavy air. "The novelist is a pain in a few political asses, too. Now . . . raise your hands."

Against my will, I raise my hands, the rifle still in my grip.

"Drop it," a guard shouts from behind Sharad, pointing his rifle toward the weapon in my arm.

I slowly lower my hands. Sharad squints at me, and I

immediately tilt the rifle upwards. The guard shouts again for me to drop the rifle. I've never shot anyone in real life. Heck, never held a gun either, much less a rifle. I pull the trigger haphazardly.

Once... twice... thrice.

Two shots fail. One hits the chandelier gleaming above his head, shaking each of its tassels. Lilting and sizzling, the ornate glass fixture collapses over Sharad. A shower of glass hits my feet. The guards jump a few steps back. I drop my gun and look at Sharad, trampled under the heavy chandelier. His head is bleeding, glass pieces have pricked his body and face. He is not moving, as if shocked... as if... dead.

I *killed* a human. Synchronous footsteps rush closer.

The auditorium's grandma clock chimes to declare 6 PM.

RASHMI AGRAWAL

Rashmi Agrawal has been published in nearly a dozen anthologies. She dreams of seeing her name on a novel's spine and is working on her first novel, a psychological thriller. She lives in India and sits by a big window to write. When she's not writing, she vexes her daughter in motherly ways. She tweets on Twitter and silently stalks her friends on Facebook here.

Twitter: @Thrivingwordss

Facebook: @rashmi.agrawal.writer

BONE MOTHER
DAPHNE FAMA

Keith's old Chevy K20 crunched over roots and rocks, leading the charge through the Osceola forest, its headlights bouncing off trees. Guns and Roses played loudly over the radio. Beer bottles open and drained to dregs rattled in the cup holders.

There were insects trilling in the woods, cicadas and frogs and all manner of nightly creatures, but they were quiet compared to the roaring of Keith's truck and Johnny's screams of vengeance.

The only thing on Keith's mind was Dolly.

Dolly, who up and left him a month ago. Who took their little boy and the stash of cash she'd made from waitressing that he'd kept safeguarded in their mattress. Dolly, who thought leaving was an option, after all the years they spent together. *That boy was his.* And what type of mother let their boy grow up without a father?

It'd taken him a full month to find out where she was hiding. He'd gone knocking on the doors of what few friends she had left. They'd been tight-lipped and hard-eyed. Full of that snake venom hate because of all the lies Dolly had stuffed them with.

It was her mother who gave her up. Directed him to a women's shelter in Jacksonville and told him to make it right. No boy should grow up without his Daddy.

Keith promised he would. And he meant it. He'd get Dolly and his boy back even if it meant torching that cult to the ground.

But once he got to Jacksonville, Dolly was already gone. It took another few weeks to find out where she and the boy had gone. She'd been swept up in some commune outside the city. In the thick Osceola Forest, between Jacksonville and Lake City.

A haven for women who'd left their husbands high and dry.

And that was all it took. Once he told his buddies that there was a commune of women living out in the woods, not a gun or man in sight, they'd been happy to drive their trucks Eastward and follow him into the woods. They were simple like that, his boys. But the end justified the means.

Now their trucks were a caravan of lights and men who could already taste the blood in the water.

A mile from the commune, Keith stopped his truck, killed the engine and jumped out with Johnny following right behind.

"What, we're walking there?" Boone called through the open window of his truck. But a grin split his lips, showing off the jagged yellow teeth between his thin lips.

Irritation burned the edges of Keith's blood. He didn't have patience for weak, lazy men. Men who only moved when stronger men led, who needed to be insulted and shamed into action. Boone let his woman go but five years before, and he'd been on a downward slope ever since.

"You want them to know we're here?" Keith shouted back. "They'll just go running deeper into the woods. Better to catch them unaware."

Boone slid out of his truck, a hand wrapped around a Marlin rifle. "You don't want to hunt them down? Bet they'd be prettier than hunting deer. White flank through the forest. "Bang, bang!" He lifted the rifle and mimed a shot, a wild drunken laugh punctuating the kill.

Keith spat, but the image kicked up a surge of pleasure in the base of his stomach. "Let me get Dolly first, and you can hunt the rest. Don't know how much of a hunt it'll be. Bunch of women, making daisy chains and braiding each other's hair in the woods. Bet they get tired ten yards out."

Three of his other boys — all drinking buddies — unloaded their guns and flashlights. The woods stretched before them, thicker and denser than it had been at the forest's entrance, but none of them were deterred. They'd all grown up hunting bucks through the panhandle. A rite of passage. Didn't matter that the swamp here was thick, wet, and mean. They were meaner.

The men followed Keith off the sparse dirt road and into the trees. Without the radio, the noise of the forest reared up all around them. Crickets chirped loudly, insects buzzed and assaulted their faces as their boots crushed leaves and slogged through wet patches of swamp, grabbing at their ankles and sometimes their knees. The half-moon provided just enough light to keep themselves from tripping over each other. They forged onward and, not for the first time, Keith wondered if that old trick on the corner outside the women's shelter had given him bad information.

Maybe she sent him on a goose hunt just to score an easy hundred dollars. If there wasn't a house full of women waiting for him at the end of this swamp, he'd go back and wrap his hands around her throat and squeeze until her head popped off.

The five of them fell silent the further they got from the truck, falling into old hunting patterns. Mouths shut, ears pricked and listening.

Their boots sloshed through the water. The forest and all its creatures turned quiet. But it wasn't *still*.

Keith slowed as eyes were still adjusting to the dark, but he was certain he could see shadows moving between the trees. Not the fast, jerky movements of rabbits or deer. But the soft, fluid movement of something intelligent.

A splash echoed behind him, followed by a sick, vicious thump. Keith turned. There in the water next to him was one of his boys. Joseph lay face down in the shallow water, his hat thrown off to reveal a dark, wet streak on the back of head.

In the moonlight, Keith could make out the figure of a woman standing over Johnny, naked and triumphant. But Keith's eyes didn't stray from the hammer in her clenched hand. Keith fired his rifle at her chest before she could lift it again. She staggered backwards, her hand covering the bright ruby he'd put in her chest.

Chaos untangled around them.

The surrounding shadows unfurled and emerged from the trees. What looked like a dozen women, young, old and naked, swarmed from the underbrush as if they'd been laying in wait. As if they knew the men would come along this path.

They descended on Keith and his hunting troupe. Knives and hammers caught the glint of light that poured from someone's flashlight. The men opened fire, shooting wildly at the wall of flesh.

For every mud-streaked woman that fell to a bullet, countless more came to take her place. Their faces had little in common save for the rage that turned their mouths to snarls and narrowed their eyes into something raw and primal.

Keith thought he was well acquainted with hate. But what he'd had in his heart for Dolly was a pale, pathetic thing to the dark rage of the women who attacked upon his boys. They tore rifles from callused hands, smashing elbows and wrists with hammers and axes.

It didn't matter how many times the men pulled their triggers. They couldn't reload fast enough.

"Oh, fuck this. Fuck this," Johnny muttered into the pandemonium before sprinting past the tangle of bodies bearing down on Boone and the rest of the boys. But the women were on him in moments, dragging him down into the waters, forcing his face into the brackish waters. Three sets of hands pressed his face and back into the suffocating muck.

More were coming all the time. Women and girls, wild-haired with the moon in their eyes, emerging from the brush and shadows between trees as if they were part of the forest.

Keith and his men were utterly surrounded. Johnny had stopped struggling. A thin stream of air bubbles popped around his ears. Boone gasped and panted on his back, his hands and arms mangled by the dull blade of an ax.

Keith lifted his gun, swinging it in a wide arc as if that might slow the tide of women tightening the circle around him.

"Keep the fuck back."

Crack.

The blow that came to the back of his head hurt for a moment, then he was down like a cow stunned before slaughter.

Dazed and waterlogged, Keith blinked up at the faces above him. With thick rope they bound his arms to his chest. By the time he'd come back to his senses enough to struggle, he was being pulled by the ropes around his ankles, his body sliding along through the swamp. And he wasn't alone. The rest of his boys were coming along with him, it seemed. He could hear them moaning and cussing and shouting for help, along with the sounds of their heavy bodies being dragged through the mud.

Keith bounced along with them, his clothes and skin catching on stone and root, which scoured and scraped exposed skin and ripped at his clothes. He bent his head away from the underbrush, but his face was flayed pink with new drops of blood forming along thick scratches.

They'd dragged him until the water gave way to soft mud and reeds. It could have been a mile, or longer, he couldn't tell. But by the time the swamp gave way to dry ground, he was certain that there wasn't an inch of skin left on his back.

Firelight that lit up the trees around him. He sputtered out a cry for help, eyes wide with fear as he caught the glint of a dozen bonfires built around not a house, but a village. Little wooden houses with roofs covered in Spanish moss. Fossilized chicken feet hung over the doors like charms. And there were women, of course. Not the dozen Keith had expected, but what looked like over one hundred women. Children played amongst themselves, but the moment the hunting party broke through the tree line, they were running towards their mothers and sisters, their faces lit up with excitement.

Soon the children wheeled around him, jumping and shouting with a fearsome joy. Among them was his boy, Liam. But his little son, who'd grown pudgy in the time he'd been taken away, looked at him as if was a stranger.

Terrified, desperate, Keith managed a plea. "Please, help me."

"Please, help me," the children echoed back. Liam's voice intertwined with their call.

At the edge of the village, a long, thick pole had been nailed between the trees. His heart trembled in his chest. He recognized it for what it was, long before they dragged him to lie before it.

A meat pole.

He remembered how much Dolly had hated what he'd done to the big bucks he came home with. It'd been a laugh then as he and the boys strung them up by their antlers on the trees behind their house.

She had stared at them, shaking like a desiccated leaf, her eyes fixated on the bright red gashes that started between their ribs and worked their way down their empty stomachs. She told him she could feel their glossy eyes on her when she was in the kitchen. It didn't matter if the curtains were pulled or not.

But it looked like sometime between then and now she'd gotten over that fear.

Boone had arrived before him, him and one of Johnny's boys. Two women stuffed cloves of garlic and fistfuls of leaves into Boone's mouth. A metal prop kept his yellow teeth from bearing down on their fast, efficient fingers. Not that he could fight back, not by the look of him. Boone had gone pale, his mangled arms weeping blood. He'd be dead before the night was done if he was lucky.

An old, large woman came for him next. She grabbed Keith by the nose, her strong callused thumb pushing down into the lower cartilage so hard he gasped. The first metal prop slipped in between his teeth. The ones dentists used were latex, softer than this, and he'd been well familiar with them because of his staunch refusal to keep his mouth open. But the one that bit into his gums now wasn't the type used on the living. His tongue recoiled against the taste of metal and something tangy and vile. He tried to jerk away, but she grabbed his nose again, keeping him in place while she roughly inserted the second.

She slapped the top of her thighs and moved on to Johnny, who'd been dragged in behind him. Johnny hadn't drowned in the water, he hadn't been that lucky. He whimpered and pleaded with the old woman, but she said nothing, her face blank, as if he was a pig squealing in an abattoir. Keith's face flushed, and his tongue moved uselessly around his mouth. Johnny hadn't done anything wrong. Hadn't hurt no one. He didn't deserve whatever was coming.

"Hey, Keith."

Dolly stood at Keith's feet. Keith struggled to sit up, but she kicked at his ribs. He stilled and realized he was afraid. Dolly had never raised her voice to him. Had never so much as laid a finger on him. But her boot in his ribs was final.

"Wouldn't move if I were you, Keith. They don't like it when the man meat moves around or starts to get ideas." Dolly laughed.

"We knew you were coming. Men like you, they always come chasing, don't they? I knew you wouldn't have the stones to come alone. But it's good timing. The last batch of boys we've gone and eaten up. And we got plenty of mouths here to feed."

She rolled her head towards the crowd of children looking on with anticipation. Their smiles cast a dismal shadow as Boone and Johnny's mouths were stuffed, and their clothes cut and peeled from their bodies.

"It takes two to four days, Keith. That's how long meat should hang before it's ready to butcher. You told me that."

Dolly knelt in front of him, her eyes black like the space between stars. She looked different than when she left him. It wasn't just the dirt on her face or the tan of her shoulders. It was those cold eyes. She never looked him in the eyes before.

She'd always averted her gaze, stared at some place over his shoulder as if he was the sun and he'd burn her eyes out.

But she stared at him now, without a hint of reverence or respect.

And he'd been wrong. She wasn't wearing a daisy crown. It was a crown of bones. Thin enough he mistook it for an animal's at first. But the longer he stared, the more he knew those dark, grungy bones must be human. Maybe bits of hand or broken tibia, bound together with twine.

A new wave of rage ripped through him, and he jerked in his ropes. A violent maelstrom that sparked a bit of that old, electric fear in Dolly's veins.

Dolly's hands clenched to fists as she stared down at him, refusing to break her gaze. Refusing to give him the satisfaction of letting him think he'd won. She'd learned that bruises fade, but the wound he'd left on her soul was slow healing. The think-you-forgot-'til-you-dream type.

She let him struggle for a moment longer before moving closer, letting her shadow wash over him, so that she was all he could see. The smell that haunted her, that old sour smell of alcohol and cheap, over-scented deodorant floated up to her. But before dawn, it would all be washed away.

She inhaled, letting all the phlegm and mucus caught in her throat, all the curses and hexes and hate, build up into a sticky mass. She spat it on his face, into his bloodshot eyes.

He'd spent years trying to eat her alive. Taking her joy and spirit piece by piece. But now it was her turn.

DAPHNE FAMA

Daphne Fama is a queer Filipina woman who traded the swamps of Florida for the mountains of South Korea. When she's not hiking the ranges with her dog she's searching out haunted places. She can be found on Twitter.

Twitter: @DaphneFama

SLEEP TIGHT
TYLER WITTKOFSKY

December 31st, 2006

    Fifteen-year-old MaryAnne Callaway was drowning in the tides of life. She was a young woman plagued by her mental illness. Her thoughts constantly revolved around death and the possibility of dying. She panicked over the little things. Her heart would nearly beat out of her chest, pound against her breastplate as anxiety consumed her. She lived in fear of her father, who had beaten her from the time she was born. He would always say it was his way of purging the sin out of her, whatever that was supposed to mean.

    She had prayed to God countless times, asking him to take the pain away, to free her from the prison she lived in, but no matter how many times she prayed or how *hard* she prayed, the punches still came. Man after man abused her frail frame, taking advantage of the fact that she couldn't stand up to them. Like a stick in the ocean, she floated helplessly.

    MaryAnne was raised to be a believer and follower of Christ with a strong Southern Baptist upbringing deep in the woods of Leland, North Carolina. They baptized her shortly after birth as a way for her father to cleanse her future sins and the sins of her mother, who had run off with another man right after MaryAnne was born. Little did the world know that her father was one of the biggest sinners of them all.

One night, during one of her father's drunken rampages, MaryAnne came to a realization that would change her life: God obviously didn't love her enough to free her from this Hell on Earth. The Church had taught her to fear God, but what kind of Creator would want to be feared? What kind of Creator would commit genocide upon his entire creation in one giant tantrum? Maybe Lucifer wasn't the bad guy after all. Maybe he was the rebellious angel, the one who condemned what his father was doing. Maybe he stood up to his father and was vilified for it.

As her father yelled her name over the sound of the television, MaryAnne slid off the side of her bed and onto her knees. Her golden blonde hair hung down the front of her white sleeping gown as she bowed her head. She closed her eyes, interlocking her hands together. "Dear Lucifer . . ." Her body trembled as the name left her lips. She opened her eyes and paused as she reconsidered her decision. Was this really what she wanted? To turn to the darkness to escape the darkness?

Fists banged on MaryAnne's locked door. "MaryAnne Louise Callaway, you open this got-damn door right now!" her father shouted, his scruff voice plagued by thirty years of smoking cigarettes.

MaryAnne closed her eyes and bowed her head again. "Dear Lucifer," she started again, getting the words out of her mouth a little quicker this time. "Please save me from my daddy. Please help me escape this."

The banging got louder and the door handle jerked back and forth. The door casing shook under the pressure. "Let me in 'fore I bust this door down!"

"Please, Lucifer!" MaryAnne cried out. Almost immediately after she said the words, a crack of lightning struck a tree just outside her window and lit up the room, followed by the loud roar of thunder. Rain pounded against the window of her small bedroom. Once the light disappeared and her eyes readjusted to the darkness, she could make out the figure of a man standing in front of her.

His jet black hair caressed his broad shoulders, covering his black Armani jacket embroidered with a red 'L' on the chest. MaryAnne looked up into his dark eyes. They seemed to be a mix of black, gray, and white spinning in fluid circles. The strange man rolled his shoulders and cracked his neck. He smiled, dagger-like teeth revealing themselves. "You rang?" he said in a baritone voice.

Stunned, MaryAnne's jaw dropped open. She couldn't believe what — *who* — stood in front of her. Lucifer. Satan. The Devil.

The banging grew louder as her father's shouting boomed through the door. Her legs shook as the thought of her father sliding his belt off his waist and unzipping his pants ran through her mind. Tears slipped from her clenched eyes. She was ready to make a deal with the true purveyor of darkness.

"Speak, child," Lucifer demanded, his voice echoing against the walls of MaryAnne's tiny bedroom.

MaryAnne looked down at her feet. "I want to get away from my daddy."

"How do you plan on doing that, child?" he asked as he stroked his chin with the tips of his black nails. "How can I, Lucifer Morningstar, help you get away from your daddy?"

Before she could speak, the sound of her father beating on the door interrupted the conversation. Lucifer looked over at the door and back at MaryAnne. "One moment," he said coolly. He walked to the door and opened it.

"Who the fu —" MaryAnne's father started.

Lucifer waved his hand in her father's beat-red face. "Sleep." The man's eyes closed and his body fell to the floor like a rag doll. Lucifer looked back at MaryAnne and smiled. "Do go on, child."

MaryAnne looked at her father's limp body. Was he dead? If he was, she didn't care. Part of her felt relieved that her father appeared to be dead. The other part of her was terrified at the magic she had just witnessed. She shook her head and looked back to Lucifer's menacing smile. "I want to be a famous singer and to travel the world. Get out of this town and away from him," she spat, pointing her tiny hand at her lifeless father.

His smile widened. "MaryAnne Callaway, famous . . . What kind of music do you sing, MaryAnne?"

"Country, sir," MaryAnne said as a smile formed on her lips. It was the first time she had smiled a genuine smile in years. It felt good. Smiling warmed her body. A feeling of hope grew within her like a candle flame in the darkness.

"Very good, as long as you don't make up some bullshit song about beating me in a fiddle competition. Which, by the way, never happened." Lucifer chuckled. He looked down at MaryAnne and stroked her cheek with the side of his finger. "I can help you achieve that, child. However, there is a catch."

"Anything, sir. I will do anything to get out of here," MaryAnne pleaded and interlocked her hands together. "I am begging you. Please help me."

"I will help you, but in fifteen years, when you are thirty years old, I will send a demon to collect your soul. You will serve me for the rest of eternity. Are you sure you are willing to give up your soul to escape him?"

Her father's beatings flashed through her mind again. The abuse from her father, the sexual abuse from her teachers and classmates, the bullying from the local priest. All those years. All that suffering would end. *Here. Now.* She nodded. "Yes."

"Stand child," Lucifer said, and he held his crooked finger out, signaling for her to stand. MaryAnne slowly rose to her feet. He reached out and placed a broken fingernail in the middle of her forehead. "Hishk lomea, sycil fluio raggas eh menis." Lucifer chanted the words over and over. The swirl in his eyes quickened, and the colors blended together into a deep gray.

Lightning flashed outside as his chanting got louder. A crack of thunder shook the house. MaryAnne jolted. Lucifer threw his head back as his chanting continued. Black smoke crept out of his mouth and nostrils. Its tendrils wrapped around MaryAnne, and her whole body went cold.

MaryAnne wrapped her arms around herself as the smokey tendrils continued to surround her. They tightened their grip around her chest. It reminded her of her father's violent grip. Her chest tightened, and her breathing turned shallow and quick. Her muscles tensed and her body shook uncontrollably.

"Calm down, child!" Lucifer roared. His skin had blackened and his eyes had turned red. Bones erupted from his skull. They curved into horns atop his head. He continued his chant. MaryAnne felt her nerves relax. A warmth fluttered in her chest and spread throughout her body until she was light as a feather. She couldn't feel her legs anymore. It was like she was floating in place. She felt her head loll and her body sway back and forth like the ebb and flow of a rocking boat.

The black tendrils slowly unwound themselves from around MaryAnne's slight frame. They retreated and disappeared into the nose, mouth, and eyes of Lucifer. The rain stopped, and the raging storm outside ceased.

As MaryAnne faded in and out of consciousness, she thought she saw Lucifer cock his head slightly and smile at her.

She closed her eyes. When she opened them again, Lucifer was gone. The sound of sirens wailing in the distance filled MaryAnne's ears. She closed her eyes again, suddenly exhausted. She felt the release of her father as she smiled one more time before the world around her faded into nothingness.

Fifteen Years Later

"Ladies and gentleman, The Grand Ole Opry of Nashville is proud to present: the one, the only, MaryAnne Callaway!" A voice resounded throughout the true home of country music. The crowd erupted in applause as the lights around the stage turned on one by one until the center of the stage lit up and revealed the now thirty-year-old MaryAnne Callaway.

The cameras zoomed in as her image filled the giant screen behind her. MaryAnne looked around at the crowd, a tear forming in her eye. She had made it.

"How are we doing tonight, Nashville?" MaryAnne yelled into the microphone. The crowd erupted again, and MaryAnne smiled.

She had taken a different route in her country music career. All of her songs helped raise mental health awareness. It had been a hard path at the start, but once she gained traction, she started making a difference in the world by changing the conversation through her music.

Picking up her jet black Martin DX Johnny Cash guitar, she began playing her hit song *Where Did You Go, Momma*. She sang her heart out, tears falling as she played. It was one of the most heartfelt songs she had ever written. She made it through the song and stopped, looking out over the crowd. Thousands of people sat in the audience and cheered as they wiped their own emotions from their faces.

A stagehand ran out onto the stage and switched guitars with MaryAnne. She began strumming the Fender Telecaster to a more upbeat tune. The crowd roared as she sang the opening lyrics to her latest song, *What The Mind Needs*.

> "When the demons come to play,
> And the children get down to pray,
> We find out what the mind needs."

A roar of thunder cracked outside and the building trembled. The lights that had illuminated MaryAnne burst, showering her with sparks. The country star shrieked and covered her head, but it was too late. The metal chains holding the lights shattered, and the metal cages holding the lights crashed down on top of MaryAnne.

"Khane," Lucifer said from his throne of the naked, twisted, and contorted bodies of the most evil humans who've ever walked the Earth. "It is time to collect the soul of one Mary-Anne Callaway."

Khane, who was down on one knee, looked up at Lucifer through the hooded black robe covering his body and most of his face. His golden-obsidian eyes shone in the light as he focused on Lucifer. He pulled the hood back to reveal the sideways cross-shaped scar above his right eyebrow.

"The child you saved from her father all those years ago?" Khane asked.

Lucifer smiled his toothy smile and intertwined his long fingers. "Yes. I have plans for Ms. Callaway."

Khane knew the twisted look on Lucifer's face and what his repulsive plans were, the way Lucifer would use her as his personal slave. Khane stood, his face even with Lucifer's chest. "I'll get right on it."

"You're my best soldier, Khane. Don't let me down," Lucifer said as he leaned back against the throne of bodies. A mix of groans echoed through the halls as the faces on the bodies grimaced in pain.

"Yes, my Lord."

MaryAnne thrashed in her bed as the nightmare took hold.

Police cars pulled up to MaryAnne's childhood home. Khane rolled his neck as his cop car came to a screeching halt outside the small two-bedroom trailer.

Khane pulled out his gun and ducked behind the open door of the cop car, following the lead of the other officers who had already arrived on the scene. One called out, "Peter Callaway, come out with your hands up!"

Khane looked across the car and asked, "So what did this guy do, anyway?"

"We got an anonymous call that he was beating his daughter and..." the other officer paused. "He raped her. Repeatedly."

A chill ran down Khane's spine. There were a lot of things that didn't bother him about humans, but rape wasn't one of them. It was the ultimate evil in Khane's eyes, something he despised as human as well. Most demons had lines they would not cross, something they deemed irreprehensible, and rape was one of Khane's.

Khane shook his head and cleared the doubt clouding his mind. He had a task to complete.

The officer who had spoken before called out again. "Peter Callaway, this is your last warning! Come out with your hands up!"

Khane patiently waited for the man to come out so he could go inside to find MaryAnne. He had to be careful because any interruption in the dream would cause MaryAnne to wake up, and he would lose his chance to take her soul.

MaryAnne laid on the floor of her childhood room. She slowly blinked and looked around at the room. She could see red and blue lights flashing through her window. In the light, she caught the unconscious figure of her father sprawled across the floor. Seeing him again, even in a dream, caused her to break down into tears.

She struggled to stand, but her legs were weak from years of trauma and abuse. As she grabbed onto the door handle to pull herself up, she heard the police calling her dad's name. She stumbled out of the room and towards the shouting.

The white trailer door was barely hanging on to the doorframe. It creaked when she opened it and was greeted by the police force readying their guns. But not as a child. In her dream, MaryAnne was thirty-years-old though she was still in the white sleeping gown from that night, exactly what she was wearing when she met Lucifer.

Like that night, her face was full of tears and stains littered her clothing. Her hair was a mess, her body covered in bold blue bruises. The demon and other officers shuddered when they saw the fear in her eyes.

MaryAnne looked around as she held up her hand to shield her eyes from the spotlights pointed at her. She was timid and scared. She cried and collapsed to the ground. She laid on her side with her knees pulled to her chest as the tears poured down her face.

"Khane," the commanding officer called out. "Go help the girl."

Khane holstered his pistol and ran up to where MaryAnne was lying. He knelt down and looked at her. If he had a heart, it would have grown at that moment. Something about this beautiful woman looking so broken and defeated tugged on Khane's consciousness and black soul.

She opened her eyes and looked into the golden-sunshine-covered-in-darkness that were Khane's eyes. Confusion overtook her as she realized this wasn't the officer who had come to her aid that night.

Khane lifted her up in his arms and brought her to his chest, touching her cheek with the back of his hand. In that instant, her eyes shot open and her body stiffened in Khane's arms as MaryAnne relived the first fifteen years of her life. She saw the moment her mother abandoned her, and the first time her dad hit her. She heard the words hurled at her throughout her life. *Whore. Slut. Piece of shit.* She had been called everything in the dictionary.

She saw the moment her father touched her inappropriately for the first time at just three years old, the first time her pastor touched her when she was five years old, and the first time her father raped her at eight years old. Nearly every man in her life, from her father to her pastor to her gym teachers, had forcibly abused her. Sold to the highest bidder to earn her keep.

She saw the moments she spent kneeled down praying to God for help. The countless nights where He was silent and watched her suffer alone. That fateful moment when fifteen-year-old MaryAnne Callaway turned to Lucifer to escape her own version of Hell.

This poor woman went through more in her first fifteen years than anybody deserved to go through. It was at that moment, through the mind of MaryAnne Callaway, that the dream demon known as Khane would experience emotion for the first time.

A tear burned in his eyes as MaryAnne gazed up at him. She could see the struggle in his eyes, a confusion she couldn't understand. As his nose and eyes twitched, the corners of his mouth turned down. Whatever was going through this man's mind, scared MaryAnne.

"Who are you?" MaryAnne asked Khane.

"A mere figment of your imagination," Khane smiled gently at her. "Wake up," he said, and snapped his fingers.

MARYANNE'S EYES shot open and she attempted to sit up in bed. Her manager, Jason, and a few of her band members sat around her in the small, sterile-looking room. Jason jumped out of his chair and ran to her side. He put his strong arm around her and rubbed her back with his soft hands.

"Breathe, MaryAnne, breathe," he whispered to her.

"Where am I?" MaryAnne asked as she looked around at the machines hooked up to her arms.

"Nashville General Hospital. You've been unconscious for a day or so now," Jason responded as he blew a strand of his long, unkempt red hair out of his face.

MaryAnne reached up and felt the bandages wrapped around her head. She winced as she pushed against them. "What happened?"

"Freak accident at the Opry," Frank, her drummer, said as he stood and walked to MaryAnne's other side. "Lightning blew a breaker and caused an explosion that broke the chains holding the lights above you."

"Doctors weren't sure if you were going to make it, MaryAnne," Jason said. "Those light cages were damn near five hundred pounds. I'm not even sure how you're awake right now, to be honest."

"I feel sore, but that's it," MaryAnne said as she wrapped her arms around herself. "I had the dream again."

"Of that night?" Jared, the guitarist, asked from the corner, glancing up from his phone to join the other two men in looking at her. They knew about the night her dad got arrested, but they didn't know about the deal she made with Lucifer. She'd told no one about how she had survived her father.

MaryAnne had met the three a few years after that night. They had been the only men in her life to respect her as a women and not treat her like a sex toy. This helped her to trust again, gave her hope, and helped her restore her faith in humanity by treating her with nothing but kindness and respect. They knew all of each other's darkest secrets. Well, almost all of them.

"Yeah, but something was different this time," MaryAnne said. "The officer who came to my aid was different this time."

"MaryAnne, do you really think you remember exactly what the man looked like?" Jared asked and pressed his thumb below his forest green eyes.

"I used to have this same dream every night. I think I have a pretty good idea of what he looks like," MaryAnne spat. Jared threw his hands up and sat back in his chair.

"You haven't had that dream in years, though," Frank interjected. "Maybe your mind is finally letting go of what happened."

MaryAnne shook her head. "I'm telling you, there was something different about this officer. Something felt different. It was like he was real and not part of the dream."

She watched as Jason chewed on his bottom lip, his ice-blue eyes full of concern. "MaryAnne, maybe you should lay back, love."

MaryAnne furrowed her brow and pouted at Jason. "Why?"

"You've bumped your head, and now you're talking crazy." Jared ran his hand through his long brown hair. "I'm sure getting hit isn't letting you think clearly so your dreams are pretty clouded."

Frank ran a hand over his mouth and down the stubble that made up his chin. "MaryAnne, let's talk about this more after the doctors check you out."

MaryAnne bit the bottom of her lips and nodded in agreement. She leaned back against the pillow and closed her eyes. She couldn't fall back asleep, but the darkness calmed her restless mind.

KHANE BOWED before Lucifer and came face to face with the decaying Stalin. The corpse's head mouthed "Help me" to Khane, so the dream demon pulled his hood down to cover his eyes further. He looked up at Lucifer and spoke. "Lord Lucifer, I don't believe we should take MaryAnne Callaway's soul."

Without looking down, Lucifer responded. "Khane, I don't really care what you *believe*. I am the Lord of Hell. I make the decisions."

Khane stood to face Lucifer. "My Lord, she went through more in the first fifteen years of her life than any of our demons ever could have imagined in their entire life." Khane's breathing increased as his nose flared. He knew he was pushing the limits with his Lord, even if Khane was the highest ranking demon in Lucifer's army.

"Which makes her prime to serve beside me as my Queen." Lucifer smiled.

"You mean your slave?" Khane spat and threw his hood off his head.

Lucifer lunged at Khane and backhanded him across the face, sending the dream demon tumbling across the floor. Khane grabbed at his face. His scar burned and throbbed in pain. "Watch your tone when you speak to me, dream demon."

Khane breathed heavily as he stared at Lucifer through his good eye. "Yes, my Lord."

"Good. Now go find the girl and bring her soul to me. If you fail again, it will be your last failure, Khane." Lucifer said and turned away from Khane.

MaryAnne sat in her hospital bed for the next few days, setting an alarm on her phone to ensure she only slept for an hour or two at a time to avoid dreaming. She needed to sleep more, but she couldn't. Something was off about the dream she had after being knocked unconscious. She couldn't put her finger on exactly what, but it had to do with the strange man. It left her with an eerie feeling in her gut.

Even after talking to the doctors, they confirmed that everything, much to their surprise, looked fine with her head. No damage to the brain, no blood clots, just a hairline skull fracture. She didn't even have a concussion. It was like something had protected her brain the whole time.

But how?

MaryAnne didn't understand. Her miraculous escape made little sense. She felt like it was connected to the golden-eyed officer somehow, but couldn't figure out how. *Or why.*

Suddenly, the realization sunk in. She shot up in the bed and looked over at Jason, who had dozed off in a chair in the far corner of the room. "Jason," MaryAnne panted.

Jason opened his eyes as he jerked his head back and up into an alert position. "What's wrong, MaryAnne?" he asked. He blinked his eyes rapidly. "Are you okay?"

"What day did the accident happen?" MaryAnne asked.

"At the Opry?" Jason asked as he sat forward and propped his elbows on his knees. MaryAnne nodded. "It was Friday."

"No," MaryAnne said, frustrated. "What was the date?"

"The 31st of December. Why?" Jason stood and took a few steps towards MaryAnne before it dawned on him. "Oh, shit. That's the night."

The room started to spin. MaryAnne's breathing increased and she brought her knees to her chest. She wrapped her arms around her knees, interlocking her fingers together and pushing her forehead into the space between her knees. Her body felt hot as she began to shake with fear.

Jason ran to her side and placed his arm around MaryAnne. "Shhh, MaryAnne. Easy love," he said. But MaryAnne couldn't calm down. Her breathing grew rapid and shallow.

"Doctor! Nurse! Somebody!" Jason called out before turning his attention back to MaryAnne and stroking her hair. "Relax. Breathe for me, love. Breathe," he whispered into her ear. He turned back to the open door and screamed once more. "Somebody! Please help!" When no one replied, Jason took off running down the hallway.

A few moments later, heavy footsteps enter the room. "Jason, I'm fine," MaryAnne said in between sniffles. Silence filled the air around her and MaryAnne lifted her head up.

Her heart nearly stopped as she locked eyes with the golden-obsidian eyes of Khane. He stood in his black robe, its hood covering his forehead. He ran his hand through his shaggy black hair, pulling back the hood to reveal the scar on his head.

"It's you," was all MaryAnne could muster.

Khane smiled gently and turned his head slightly to the side. His eyes never left hers. He took another step forward, careful not to startle her and break the dream he had created in MaryAnne's brief sleep. He had to see her again. He had to save her.

"Who are you?" MaryAnne finally managed to ask.

"Khane," he said, his scruffy voice echoing in the small hospital room.

"What do you want from me? Where is Jason?" she cried out and kicked the covers off of her.

"Jason is fine. He's sleeping. So are you," Khane said and took another two steps towards MaryAnne.

"What do you mean *I'm sleeping*, I'm clearly awake," MaryAnne yelled as she shifted nervously. She tried to get out of the bed but her limbs were paralyzed.

"You're dreaming. I'm a dream demon," Khane confessed.

MaryAnne started sobbing and shaking again. "No, please. Don't take me yet. Let me at least say goodbye to the people I love."

"I'm not taking your soul, MaryAnne. I'm trying to protect you," Khane said. He reached her bed, took her hand in his, and gently rubbed the top with his thumb.

MaryAnne looked from their interlocked hands to Khane's

glowing eyes and back down at their hands. "Why would you want to protect me?" she asked.

"You went through so much in the first fifteen years of your life. You did what you had to do. I won't let you go back to the same Hell you've already experienced," Khane said, squeezing her hand and bringing it to his lips. "When I was human, my birth mother was raped and killed. I can't let you go back to that."

"You're lying! Tell me the truth!" MaryAnne screamed as she jerked her hand away. Khane stumbled backwards as rips in the ether began forming and the dream started to fall apart.

"I am telling you the truth MaryAnne! Lucifer will send another demon once he realizes I failed to retrieve your soul." Khane shouted back. A gust of wind swirled through the hospital room. Khane braced himself against a wall as it pushed him backwards.

"You're lying!" she shouted again.

Khane struggled to take a step forward. "Listen to me, MaryAnne. You have to calm down." Khane tried to take another step forward, using all of his energy to do so. "I can protect you, but you have to trust me."

"NO!" She shrieked, covering her ears with her hands.

MARYANNE SCREAMED. Her eyes shot open as she woke from the nightmare. Jason and Jared jumped out of their chairs and ran to her side. Each man got to one side of her and gently rubbed her back, whispering that everything was alright, and it was just a dream.

Jason brushed her hair out of her face "Same dream?"

MaryAnne shook her head. "No. It was the same man, but

he was here, in the hospital. He said he was a demon, but he was trying to protect me from Lucifer."

Jared and Jason glanced at each other and back at MaryAnne. "Maybe the nurse should lower your pain meds, MaryAnne," Jared said. "Your dreams are becoming more and more bizarre."

"No, you don't understand!" MaryAnne sobbed. "That night, the night the police arrested my dad, I made a deal with Lucifer. He would own my soul after fifteen years if he saved me from my dad and helped me become a famous country music star. Now, they've come to collect my soul." She paused as tears streamed down her cheeks. "I'm going to die."

Jason bit his chapped bottom lip. "MaryAnne, demons don't exist. You're talking rubbish, love."

"No," MaryAnne said as she swatted the two men away from her. "Listen to me. I am telling the truth!"

A few nurses ran to the small room, crowding around her and beginning to check her vitals. A man pushed his way through the crowd. He stood a good foot taller than the rest. It was the lead doctor that had been looking after MaryAnne since she arrived.

"Nurse," the man shouted as he turned to a young blonde woman behind him. "Get a 5cc bag of saline for her IV and get her a stabilizer." He pushed up the bridge of his glasses and looked back at the two men standing near MaryAnne. "What happened?"

"They won't believe me!" MaryAnne screamed out as she thrashed in the bed, now being restrained by Jared and Jason.

"She woke up yelling and rambling about a demon trying to steal her soul," Jason said through gritted teeth as he wrestled with MaryAnne to keep her down.

The doctor stroked his chiseled chin and ruffled through the chart in his hands. "Interesting. Let's get her sedated. I want to run a few additional tests. The hit may have taken more of a toll than we initially thought."

A nurse ran into the room with a bag of clear liquid. She hung it on the IV stand beside MaryAnne's bed, attached the tube to her catheter, and injected something into her IV.

MaryAnne kicked and screamed for a little bit longer, but eventually, her movements became less violent and less frequent. "Please, don't let me fall asleep," she begged anyone who would listen. "Please . . ." she mumbled as her eyes closed and she drifted off into a deep sleep.

MARYANNE OPENED her eyes and looked to her left. She was still in her hospital room. It was quiet. Almost too quiet. She turned her head to the right and saw a cloaked figure in a chair in the far corner. The figure looked up and she was met with those familiar golden-obsidian eyes.

She tried to scream but couldn't open her mouth. She tried to move her body but had no control. The only thing she could do was move her head, blink, and breathe. She closed her eyes and shook her head back and forth. She tried to roll her body out of the bed to escape the dream demon sitting across from her to no avail. When she finally stopped and opened her eyes, Khane was standing at her bedside. Her heart beat against the inside of her chest as panic set in.

"I'm not trying to hurt you." Khane sighed as he pulled his hood back. "Please, just calm down and listen to me."

It wasn't like MaryAnne had a choice. Her breathing deepened as anger boiled within. She squinted at him and tried to spit. All she could manage was a glob inside of her mouth, but she couldn't part her lips to spit it at him.

"I don't want to hurt you, MaryAnne. Please listen. We have to get you out of this hospital. You're an easy target here," Khane said as he kneeled down next to her and took her hand in his. "I want to save you."

MaryAnne, for the first time since she had met him, took in Khane's words. Not just heard them, but truly understood the meaning behind them. The man who was supposed to destroy her was the one who wanted to save her. How could she believe this demon was truly trying to help her, though? He was, after all, a demon sent by Lucifer.

She shook her head as much as she could. Khane snapped his fingers and MaryAnne felt the pressure leave her lips. She opened her mouth and spoke. "I can't understand or believe that a demon would want to help *me*, of all people. I was nobody before I became famous, and I'll be nobody after I die."

"Because I've seen your pain and suffering, MaryAnne," Khane said to her, his golden-obsidian eyes locked with hers. "I've seen what you went through, and it's more than anybody should ever have to go for. You're special MaryAnne, and you deserve this shot at life."

"You're willing to sacrifice your life for me?" MaryAnne asked honestly. She couldn't understand how something so evil was so willing to help her, to risk everything just to free her.

"I am," Khane confirmed as he brought her hand to his lips and kissed it softly. "I've lived a long time. I've done a lot of things, some good and some not so good. I'm willing to sacrifice myself to help you. Think of it as my redemption song."

"How do you plan on saving me from Lucifer?" MaryAnne asked.

Khane pinched the bridge of his nose and took in a deep breath. "I'm not sure yet. I can protect you from the other demons for now. I'll figure out Lucifer later. Right now, we have to get you out of this place."

"My dream or the hospital?"

"Both," Khane said as lightning flashed outside. The two shielded their eyes from the light. When MaryAnne opened her eyes, they were no longer alone in the dream.

"Khane, you've failed," a voice called from the shadows. Fire roared around the figure as she stepped out of the shadows as she cracked her neck. "You need to return to Hell and face punishment."

"I won't be returning to Hell anytime soon, Kael," Khane said with a coolness in his voice that chilled MaryAnne. "It would be in your best interest to leave."

"I'm here to collect her soul," Kael said. "And I don't intend on leaving before I do."

"Then you won't be leaving," Khane said and pulled a dagger from his robe pocket. The powder white blade was carved from the bone of an angel. It was one of the few weapons that would kill a demon.

Khane turned to MaryAnne. "You need to wake up, now."

MaryAnne squeezed her eyes shut and willed herself to wake up. Shaking in the bed and thinking 'wake up' over and over again did her no good. When she opened her eyes, she still saw Khane by her bedside and Kael standing in the shadows. "I can't wake up!"

Khane looked at her and snapped his fingers. "Wake up." Nothing happened. MaryAnne remained in bed. No tears in the fabric of the dream appeared. She truly couldn't wake up.

"They sedated her in the hospital, Khane," Kael mocked with a slight chuckle. "She isn't going anywhere except to Hell."

"ENOUGH!" Khane shouted. He turned back to face Kael.

"I'm done with these games, Kael. If you want the girl's soul, you have to go through me."

Kael laughed at Khane's challenge. "We know how this is going to go." She interlocked her fingers and pushed her hands outwards. Each of her knuckles popped in unison. The demon pulled out a black blade similar to Khane's, but made with demon bones, powerful enough to seriously wound a demon but not kill one. She twirled it in between her fingers and smiled at Khane.

The dream demon readied himself in a battle stance. He slid one foot in front of the other, knees slightly bent, hands in front, blade pointed out.

Kael lunged at Khane. He sidestepped and she crashed into the wall behind him. The demon-bone blade fell to the ground and slid across the room. Khane grabbed Kael by her hair and tossed her into the wall on the opposite side of the room.

"I don't want to hurt you, Kael," Khane said as he circled her.

Kael pushed herself up with one arm and stared at Khane. "Funny, because that's exactly what I want to do to you." She propelled herself towards Khane and knocked him to the ground.

Khane slammed his fist into Kael's nose. As she grabbed her face, Khane shoved her off of him and kicked her across the room. Her body smashed into a clothes cabinet and lay there motionless.

He walked over to her and she threw her legs out and knocked Khane backwards. As he stumbled, Kael popped up and struck Khane in the side of the face.

Khane fell backwards, landing on his back and cracking his head against the ground. Kael jumped on top of Khane and began wailing on his face. He threw his hands up to block the punches, but her assault never wavered.

MaryAnne watched the scene unfold, unable to move. She wasn't sure if it was fear or Khane's hold on her that had her body unwilling to move a muscle. Her heart beat faster with every hit Khane took.

Khane caught Kael's fist and threw her off of him. He rolled over and pushed himself off the ground. He ran to Kael and straddled her, holding her arms down with his knees.

"Enough, my sister!" Khane's voice boomed, which caused the room to shake.

Kael struggled under Khane's weight. "I'll kill you, Khane," she said through gritted teeth. "You're a traitor!"

Khane turned to MaryAnne. "Wake up!"

"I can't," MaryAnne cried.

Kael glanced over and saw Kael reach for the blade just beyond her fingertips. She quickly stretched her arm and wrapped her fingers around the hilt.

"Khane, watch out!" MaryAnne shouted.

It was too late. Kael stabbed the blade into his arm. Khane gritted his teeth as the blade burned in his arm, but he never lost his grip on his sister.

Khane snatched the blade with his free hand and ripped it from his arm. He roared in pain as he tossed the blade aside. Kael squirmed under him, but Khane snarled and sunk his blade into her chest. The life left her eyes as the blade pierced her soul, draining the life force out of her. She didn't even have time to scream before she crumbled into ash.

Khane stared at the pile of ash he was kneeling on. He had killed his sister in arms. His breathing increased the more he thought about his actions.

He turned back to MaryAnne. She could see the hurt in his eyes. He put his head down and said, "Wake up."

He snapped his finger and lightning exploded within the room. The dream fell apart as tears ripped it apart. Blackness matched by the night sky revealed itself. Swirls of gray and red filled the room.

MaryAnne cried out, "Khane, don't leave me. Please."

Khane shook his head. "Get out of the hospital and hide somewhere safe. I'll find you when I can."

She reached out to him and he took her hands in his. He smiled softly, a glint of happiness shimmered in the darkness of his eyes. The care in his face radiated throughout the room despite the tumultuous state of her dream. She could see something more than care in his expression. Tears streamed down MaryAnne's face as Khane disappeared from her vision. Her hands dropped to her lap. She fought waking up, trying to bring Khane back, but nothing she was doing was working as her eyes fully shut and a flash of light filled her vision.

MARYANNE OPENED her eyes and looked around. She was in the hospital room surrounded by a sleeping Jason, Frank, and Jared. She was awake. She didn't want to be, but she was. MaryAnne knew she had to get out of the hospital and back home. At least there she had security systems and escape routes.

She slowly slid the IV out of her arm. She took a deep breath in as the cold metal slid underneath her skin. She leaned over and flipped the switch to the machine she was hooked to. The hum of the machines died down as the room darkened. She took the monitors off one by one.

MaryAnne looked around to make sure none of the men had woken up. Once she was confident they were still asleep, she rolled out of the bed and crept across the room. She grabbed her phone and wallet off of a side table and made her way toward the door, carefully opening it to avoid any sounds. Hearing the faint ping of an alarm going off at the nurse's station, she left the room and closed the door quietly behind her. Still in her hospital gown, MaryAnne bolted down the hall towards the red exit sign in the distance. Footsteps resounded behind her.

She picked up speed. Faster and faster she raced toward the exit sign. She crashed through the door and down the steps. She made her way down five flights of stairs. Pulling out her phone, MaryAnne pulled up the rideshare app. A fifteen minute wait. *That's too long.*

MaryAnne flew out of the side door of the hospital and ran to the road. She looked into the distance at the quiet skyline of a busy city. It was an eerie feeling for a town like Nashville to be so dark and quiet, even for it being late at night. Taking off down the road towards her house, she turned and held her thumb out with hope at every set of headlights she saw.

Finally, a set of headlights slowed down and pulled up to the curb next to her. She opened the back door of the car and practically fell into the seat. As she buckled her seatbelt, she heard a voice say, "Hello, MaryAnne."

MaryAnne paused and slowly looked up. She recognized that voice all too well. She caught a set of obsidian eyes staring at her in the rearview mirror.

"Lucifer."

KHANE APPEARED in the palace of Hell and stormed his way to the palace room. He kicked open the tall auburn doors and walked in. He stared at Lucifer, who was sitting with one leg on top of his opposite knee and his fingers interlocked.

"Where is she?" Khane demanded.

Lucifer ran his hands through his hair and stroked his chin. "Who?" he said and smiled down at Khane.

"Don't play games with me, Lucifer," Khane spat. He could feel his blood boiling. "Tell me where MaryAnne is."

"The soul you failed to collect?" Lucifer mocked.

Khane gritted his teeth. "I'm only going to ask once more. Where is MaryAnne Callaway?"

"She's around here somewhere," Lucifer said as he shrugged his shoulders.

Khane was tired of the games Lucifer was playing. His wings unfolded and shot out through his robe. The golden-obsidian feathers glimmered in the flames of Hell, causing Lucifer to look the other way. Each feather had the same sideways cross pattern Khane had above his eye, the shadows reflecting tiny crosses throughout the throne room.

"Enough, Lucifer," Khane boomed. "I'm here to free the girl's soul. She doesn't deserve this."

"She made a deal. She knew the consequences. Her soul is mine, Khane. She will sit beside me as the Queen of Hell for as long as I see fit," Lucifer said as he stood. His horns grew from his skull and curled up on top of his head as his wings unfurled.

Lucifer's shiny black feathers had sharp edges, looking like rows of shark teeth.

Khane watched Lucifer carefully as he stepped down the steps of his throne of bodies. Khane slid his hand into his pocket and grabbed the hilt of his angel blade. He rolled his neck and said, "She didn't agree to live in the same Hell she lived in for the first fifteen years of her life! You lied to her, and you know it."

Fire flashed in Lucifer's eyes. He flexed his wings and extended them until they filled almost the entire length of the room. "How dare you, dream demon!" Lucifer shouted. He flapped his wings and flew towards Khane.

Khane leaped into the air to avoid Lucifer. Lucifer pivoted and aimed back at Khane. Khane spun around, but it was too late. Lucifer plowed into Khane's torso and they both tumbled to the ground.

Lucifer grabbed Khane's collar and held him against the wall. "You insufferable, pestilent, vial demon." He raised his fist and brought it crashing towards Khane's face.

Khane quickly reached up and grabbed Lucifer's incoming fist. He lifted his head and stared into Lucifer's shining obsidian eyes. He brought a knee to the torso of the stunned Lucifer, causing the demon lord to let go of his grip on Khane.

Khane readied himself in a fight position with one fist raised in front of his face and the other even with his chest.

Lucifer laughed. "You're going to sacrifice your life to try and save this girl?"

"I'll do whatever I can to protect her," Khane said. "Now tell me where she is."

Lucifer snapped his fingers and a demon pushed out a cage with MaryAnne's beaten and bloodied body tied to the bars. She had cloth stuffed in her mouth, and her head hung low. When she finally looked up through swollen eyes, she saw Khane. She felt hope again.

Khane's blood boiled. "What have you done to her?" he shouted.

"Watch your tone, Khane!" Lucifer roared, smoke emitting from his flaring nostrils. "Or I'll make her tenure in eternity far less than desirable."

Khane leapt into the air with one fist behind his head. He came crashing down and landed his fist square in Lucifer's face. Lucifer flew back and slid across the ground into a wall. The wall cracked as dust and tiny Hellrocks fell around him

"If it's a fight you want, it's a fight you'll get." Lucifer stood and threw his head back and laughed as he grew in size. His muscles began spasming and shifting to a more defined and toned feature. He snapped his fingers and a giant black pitchfork appeared on his hands.

Khane took a step back, still ready in his fight position. He pulled his angel blade out of his pocket again and held it tight in his hand.

Lucifer flew headfirst at Khane, tackling him to the ground. Lucifer lifted his pitchfork above his head, but Khane threw Lucifer off and onto his back. Khane quickly jumped up and swiped at Lucifer with the blade.

Lucifer rolled out of the way of the blade and jumped to his feet. "Is that all you've got, dream demon?" Lucifer chuckled.

Khane looked over at MaryAnne who had been watching the entire exchange. A tear streaked down her cheek, breaking up the ash and soot that covered her face. Khane turned his attention back to Lucifer.

"You're going to pay for what you did to her," Khane said with a coolness in his voice. His bravery sent hope through MaryAnne as she watched his wings turn towards Lucifer.

Feathers shot out from his wings like missiles. Lucifer brought his wings around him to block them, and they scattered to the ground. When he opened his wings, he was face to face with Khane.

Khane grabbed Lucifer by the horns and smashed his face into his knee. Khane tossed him down and he rolled across the Hellstone floor.

Lucifer lifted himself up on an elbow as Khane reared back his foot. Lucifer grabbed his foot and slung Khane across the room. He crashed into MaryAnne's cage, sending it and her tumbling across the floor. Khane's angel blade slid with him and landed at MaryAnne's feet.

MARYANNE WATCHED Lucifer make his way to Khane's limp body and kick the dream demon across the floor. sending Khane flying into the side of his human throne. The bodies moaned as Khane crashed into the side of Lucifer's throne. Lucifer walked over to Khane and lifted him up by his broken wing. "The kingdom of Hell will see what happens when one of my own tries to turn on me. You will be an example they will tell stories about over the next millennia."

MaryAnne opened her eyes to see the glimmering blade in front of her. Her breath hitched. She grabbed the blade and attempted to stand, but her legs wobbled and she fell to the ground. A tear slipped down her cheek as she thought to herself. "You've got this, MaryAnne."

She opened her eyes and attempted to stand again. This time, though, she made it to her feet. She stumbled across the floor, her arms hanging at her side as she zig-zagged. Her breathing was heavy as she made her way across the throne room.

Lucifer slammed Khane into the side of the hellstone walls, causing a crack to form in the structure behind his body. MaryAnne caught a glimpse of Khane's eyes, the golden sparkle slowly fading. Her breathing quickened as she started to run.

"NO!" she shouted and drove the blade between Lucifer's wings.

Lucifer dropped Khane and roared in pain. He reached around his back to pull out the blade. Failing, he instead swiped at MaryAnne who narrowly dodged his sharp claws. Lucifer flitted around in a frenzy of anguish and rage. Mary-

Anne's breath slowed as she watched Lucifer wail and blood gushed from his wound.

MaryAnne swallowed. This was her chance. Scared though she was, she could do this. She *needed* to. She focused on Lucifer's wriggling form and then leaped up onto his back. She yanked the blade out of his back. She tottered, almost losing her balance before swiftly plunged the blade into his neck.

"Bitch..." Lucifer growled and collapsed in a pool of his own blood.

MaryAnne crouched face-to-face with the demon king. "Look at me," she spat. Lucifer's eyes refused to connect with hers. "I'm the Lord of Hell now."

With those words, MaryAnne pulled the blade from Lucifer's neck and slit his throat. His eyes bulged as blood poured from his neck. MaryAnne stood and rolled Lucifer over with her foot. She brought the blade down into Lucifer's chest and twisted when she felt it pierce his soul.

MaryAnne watched Lucifer's eyes close and his head loll. His body burst into a fit of Hellfire and burned away, leaving nothing but ashes. MaryAnne looked over at Khane as he shed a single tear, but *only* a single tear.

Soon Khane got to his feet and walked over to MaryAnne. "Your soul is now free from the contract you made with the Kingdom of Hell. Live the rest of your life and love like there is no tomorrow."

Five Years Later

MARYANNE STOOD backstage at the Grand Ole Opry in Nashville. It was the first time she had the courage to perform on that stage since her accident. Since the night she met Khane the dream demon.

She hadn't told Jason, Frank, or Jared what had happened to her in Hell. They wouldn't have believed her anyway. When she had woken, she was back in her hospital bed like nothing had ever happened. Nobody had noticed she was gone, it was as if she had slept for maybe an hour or two.

MaryAnne Callaway heard the announcer call her name. The crowd erupted. Then the giant drapes in front of her flew open. The spotlight turned on and MaryAnne appeared on a big screen behind her.

She looked out in the crowd and caught a set of golden-obsidian eyes staring at her from the crowd. She closed her eyes and smiled. "How y'all doing tonight, Nashville?" MaryAnne yelled as she threw her hand up and waved.

The crowd cheered. She strummed her guitar, and the crowd went wild again as she began to play her most recent hit, *Fight Like Hell* with Frank and Jared behind her. She played her alligator mahogany Gretsch G9240 and when she got to the chorus, the entire crowd sang along.

"*Fight like Hell,*
Don't stop going,
Keep on fighting.
Fight like Hell,

Embrace your demons,
make them friends.
Fight like Hell,
In the darkness,
There's progress.
Fight like Hell,
We're in this together,
Forever."

TYLER WITTKOFSKY

Tyler Wittkofsky is an award-winning marketing and communications professional, multi-genre author, podcaster, blogger, and mental health advocate from the southern coast of North Carolina, where he lives with his wife, Grace, and dogs, Dutch and Belle.

He started writing poetry to cope with his mental illnesses and eventually published *Coffee, Alcohol, and Heartbreak*. His first novel, *(Not) Alone*, was based on true events surrounding the struggles of living with mental illness. *The Seeds of Love: Sunflower Kisses Book One* was his debut romance novel centered on a mentally ill young man. You can find all of Tyler's social media, book, and website links on Linktree.

Linktree: @wittkofsky

THE FOUR
AKUA LEZLI HOPE

They found her. In some way Lena would never figure out, they found her. Less than a week after Lena moved with her family into their first house, three girls on bikes rang her front door bell. Her mother was pleased at the prospect of new friends. Lena wasn't. She preferred sitting in her new corner of the kitchen by the shelves of spices and flour, reading books for refuge and comfort.

"Hi," they said. "Can you come out? Come on, hang out, ride around with us for a while!"

Their names were Laney, Karen, and Melba. Laney was the shortest, plumpest, pearly tan skin covered in freckles, and curls. Karen was about an inch taller, warm amber, with her hair pulled back tightly in a red rubber-banded ponytail. Melba, the youngest by a year, was tallest with long, bronze-walnut limbs, black glasses on her sharp cheeks and her jet-black hair was ear length. Lena would fit right in, be the second tallest, a nutmeg in their brown array, with two short braids, the same age as Laney and Karen.

Their matter-of-fact introduction included asking if she

had a bike and telling her they all lived down the block, around two corners, on 137th street.

Somehow, they'd seen her or sniffed her out or something. Lena was shy but began to welcome their rescue from her mother's many demands. This was a new land of lawns and yards and oppressive sameness for Lena who had moved from the South Bronx. The girls eased an ache for her block and friends.

Lena, Laney, and Melba were older siblings with endless chores, which meant the moments stolen for bike rides were precious. Karen was a sort of only child. Adopted from Barbados by her strict aunt and uncle, she didn't have any sibling-minding duties on top of cleaning, though she was treated like cheap labor as she scrubbed and cleaned their house to gleaming perfection. With no annoying little brothers or sisters prying and digging in her business and bothering her, her time was her own once the work was done.

For fun, the four roamed the neighborhood, always on their bikes. They became handy at repair and shared tips – getting patch kits, bicycle pumps, and various-sized wrenches. When summer finally came, it was one long adventure of their own creation. Occasionally their families took them to the beach, and sometimes there were trips to Manhattan museums or the Bronx zoo, but they all said that their best times were spent in each others' company.

North, South, East, West, united we are just the best, they would chant. *West, South, North, East, together we just can't be beat.*

Before the girls, Lena's only friend was Mrs. Allmender, who was really more her mother's friend, but the older woman loved sharing books and stories with Lena. Now she had friends to share her time with, and they spent a lot of it in the empty lot across from Mrs. Allmender's house.

On the Lot was a tiny hill. Despite being in a city, there were rabbits, snakes, and tiny little frogs in the Lot. Pheasants and all sorts of birds rummaged in the scrubby bushes. There wasn't much to the Lot, just tall grasses colored by the occasional wild flower, but it was a place to pause as they circumnavigated the neighborhood. Its hill, tiny though it was, was great for sledding in the winter, and walking up and riding down all year round. As traffic was nearly non-existent in the quiet, tree-lined neighborhood, they could safely spin out into the street. The four made a place to lean, nestle, and rest at the base of the hill.

One day, when playing out on the hill, they felt something. A tremor? An earthquake? These things never happen — not in New York City, never in Queens, but they all felt it in their backs as they lay on the mound.

They turned and put their hands there where their backs had been.

"*I feel a humming,*" Karen said with her lilting accent.

"*It's weird,*" Laney said and looked at Lena, and they just both laughed.

"*Something's . . . something's there.*" Melba snatched her hand away.

Laney grabbed Melba's hand and pushed it back in place saying, "*No, keep it there! Let's see, let's see . . . feel that?*"

Lena felt the humming move through her hands, up their arms and into her chest and through her bodies. When it reached her feet, she saw the other girls all pull their hands away at the same time.

Something was in the mound. What was it? Nothing they could think of existed in Springfield Gardens before their homes were there. Before, there was nothing other than farms from the 1600s. Didn't seem like anything much to consider, though what made the tiny hill? Maybe something landed and attracted the dirt. Again, who could say? But for the first time, the four girls felt connected in a very new way, more than their similar ages or birth order or duties.

The four looked at each other and laughed because it was a tingling goodness, a kind of clarity. They could hear each other without speaking aloud! It was fluid and easy and relaxed. The sky felt clearer as if the blue was not the high-in-summer-blue, but both darker and lighter than what they looked up at and saw through the clouds. They felt they could move the plump, cottony cumulus clouds just by looking to the left or right, or up and down. It was the silent time of day for birds, but the crickets and cicadas were loud.

They began to look for little creatures to see the effect of the sudden telepathy. Scaring bugs was too easy. Lena saw a squirrel and asked it to come closer and it did. They said nothing aloud to each other, nothing at all. After a while, they grew bored. They left the Lot and resumed their small daily adventures: riding in a circumference of their neighborhood, down the steep slope to the park and around the park by Springfield Boulevard, and then back home again.

That evening they each said good night to each other in their separate rooms in their separate beds and separate homes. Something extraordinary had happened that day.

One day Lena and Laney were watching a car speed crazily down their streets. A three-year-old on a red tricycle was slowly crossing what had been the empty street. The car stopped, jerked backwards to where they had seen its speeding begin, and stalled. The two girls looked at each other and giggled. They watched as the car restarted and continued on the other way, away from the young boy.

"I wonder what happened," Lena said as she and Laney rode around slowly waiting for Melba and Karen to come out.

When Melba and Karen appeared, the two girls recounted what they'd seen.

Melba laughed. '*Oh the car, fixed it*'.

"Yeah," is all that Karen said aloud.

"We've got to do more good things," said Melba.

"Of course, of course we do," they all agreed, but they couldn't think of anything in the neighborhood to do or fix. This time when they rode, they rode, reaching, scanning, thinking, feeling for what might be amiss.

Too many beers in a hot afternoon — they ignored that. Parents screaming at some kids — they ignored that. But the next day, the girls felt something awful in the pit of all their stomachs, squirming in each of their minds. It was off their usual riding path, but not far. They knew this girl, Nilda, and with their unusual new power, they felt her pain. Visceral, deep, tormenting.

Something sad and horrible was happening to her. Something they could not name but could feel twisting within themselves. In their mind, they could see her crying and thought of inviting Nilda to bike with them. That was not a solution, though, because she would still have to return home and home was where the dark squidgy thing was, where she was being hurt. The thought of her being constantly in fear weighted upon them heavily. They had to do something.

Nilda's little brother was friends with Melba's little brother, a whiney, big-head brat. Maybe they could get something out of him when he came to play. But no, nothing came out of him, just stupid boy thoughts. They'd have to try something different. The girls were afraid to visit, to ring the doorbell but they didn't want to let her go either.

They heard her crying at night and not from spanking. Her father, they saw. Her father hurt her. In their mind, they saw

Nilda's mother, passed out when Nilda's father hurt her. The girls felt that visceral, deep pain almost every night.

How could they fix this? They thought about it together at night before they went to sleep. They considered the possibilities: Steal her, help her run away. Who could they tell, if she didn't say anything? Who could *they* tell if they couldn't say how they knew? They thought of how embarrassed Nilda would be if they ever said anything to her.

Nilda's pain radiated from blocks away, sharply and clearly. It burned their soul, wouldn't let them rest now that they knew it existed. They had to rid themselves of the pain, her pain, before it suffocated them all.

First, they tramped on it, forcing it away in their minds for what seemed like a long time, though it really was just a week. Their empathy grew louder. They had to do something.

The four girls asked each of their parents and guardians if they could have a night hangout. They picked Lena's yard, which was closest to Nilda, and offered the most privacy.

It wasn't dark until 9 p.m. in the summer, and the moment it was, the four biked over onto Nilda's street. Laney and Lena picked two points in front of the girl's house. Melba and Karen snuck to the rear of the house. The four girls began to engage with the thing that hurt Nilda through their telepathy.

They pushed at the fear and hurt. They pushed it away with all the strength they had. They struggled and struggled. It was like sticking their hands in goo and turning a key. Their arms were sucked up and trapped in a weird darkness, like quicksand or a sinkhole. The burning pain almost enveloped them, but they would not let it win. It could not overtake Nilda again. They forced it back, whatever it was, and soon it stopped. The deep terror receded. The four girls stopped Nilda from being hurt that night, but the feeling still lingered in their stomachs.

Exhausted but hopeful, they returned to their homes.

When Lena returned home, her parents were waiting. "That was a quick hangout," they said.

"Oh we got tired," Lena said and quickly departed to her room. The three made similar excuses.

THE FOUR SPENT another couple of days regaining their strength. They couldn't believe how hard it was to undo the thing, whatever it was. They were grateful there was no such thing in their fathers and guardians. There was sometimes unreasonableness or sternness but not this . . . nastiness, this indifference. They never knew such a thing existed before, but were grateful to each other to help fix it.

Lena thought that night about something Mrs. Allmender had once said. "If you're ever in trouble, think of the highest good in the brightest light. Love will always prevail." It gave Lena hope that her and her friends could become stronger and defeat the darkness holding Nilda hostage. She told the others what Mrs. Allmender had said, adding, *'we have to ignore the squishy-yechy and turn the key. We have to think about blasting it with light.'*

So they chose another night to hangout at Lena's. With all the parents' curiosity satisfied, Lena's father at work on the night shift and her mother tired from work and busy inside with the little ones, there was time enough for the four to sneak back over to Nilda's house.

They tried again, this time thinking about light and love and circling Nilda with a pointy circle that radiated light. Collectively, they formed a circle of light around Nilda from her feet to above her head until she was surrounded by light. The sounds of Nilda's father approaching resonated through their ears, and when her father came to hurt her, he was blasted down the stairs and tumbled right out Nilda's front door.

The girls gasped at the vision and their mind and bolted home.

Sirens echoed throughout the neighborhood.

Afterwards, the girls learned that the neighbors had heard the commotion, saw the bad father laying disheveled and confused on the lawn, and had called the cops. For some reason the bad father went away. It was not a totally happy ending. They couldn't fix him, and the mother was still having problems, but she got a little bit better. Nilda was still hurt, but her pain did not radiate out to them as strongly as it had before. She was again a girl. A sad girl, but a girl on her way to healing. And that's what the Four did that summer: connecting and saving, healing and using light.

AKUA LEZLI HOPE

Akua Lezli Hope uses sound, words, fiber, glass, metal, and wire to create poems, patterns, stories, music, sculpture, adornments, and peace. She wrote her first speculative poems in the sixth grade and has been in print every year, except one, since 1974 with over 400 poems published.

Her collections include Embouchure: Poems on Jazz and Other Musics (ArtFarm Press, 1995; Writer's Digest book award winner), Them Gone (The Word Works, 2018), Otherwheres: Speculative Poetry (ArtFarm Press, 2020; the 2021 Elgin Award winner), and Stratospherics (a micro-chapbook of scifaiku available from the Quarantine Public Library).

You can find her website, Instagram, and Twitter.

Website: akualezlihope.com

Twitter: @akualezli

Instagram: @specpovids

NO MOTHER OF FRANKENSTEIN
TESSA HASTJARJANTO

An old man leered at me as I hurried across the subway platform, his stare following my every footstep. He sat on the ground, surrounded by trash bags filled with all of his belongings half-hidden under a blanket. His dirty, faded coat was filled with holes that would barely keep him warm during the freezing nights. Scratching his leg, the seam of his pants rode up a little, flashing a hint of metal. The scowl on his face deepened as my eyes scanned his space. I expected him to growl at me. I raised my eyebrow. If only he understood the irony of the situation.

You'd think you'd get used to it after twelve years. People looked and stared, some even hissed or spit at me. I never wanted to be a face millions of people would recognize. News outlets used my photo without permission after the tabloids made me a public figure. I'm hardly that. Only a handful of people look at me with admiration or curiosity. I could tell they wanted to start a conversation, but they never would. Instead, they'd turn to their friends and whisper. They probably didn't even realize I can hear those whispers too.

I made my way through the throng of grumbling people to catch my ride. I was already running late, and missing my train wasn't an option. The metal doors started beeping as I pushed myself between a college freshman carrying every book for the upcoming year and a sweaty banker who had a few too many combo meals for breakfast.

The joys of the morning rush.

The banker snarled at me, but then his eyes met mine and drifted to the side of my head. His mouth snapped shut, and he looked the other way. I untucked my hair from behind my ear to cover up my temple. I hated how it looked, even with my husband's daily assurance I was beautiful, every part of me, including the little titanium node poking out.

People are scared of change. I wish they didn't take it out on me, though. They call me a freak of nature. Partially true, but it wasn't by choice. Others called me an abomination. I understood why they said these things, but not why they had to bother me with their insecurities.

The man's eyes followed me as I got off at the next stop. He wore disgust as the color of his lipstick, and there was nothing I could do to change it. He wasn't going to listen to me, a monster.

My first stop of day: getting my morning coffee. Next up was meeting with a new author I'd taken on, Ilona. I always dreaded first meetings because of all the questions. I needed this pick-me-up. As I walked into the coffee shop, Anya's smile beamed from the counter, our eyes connecting for a second before she went back to helping the other customers.

"Good morning," she said as I reached the front of the line. "Your usual, Mrs. Perez?"

"Yes, and please call me Olivia," I said.

"Oh, I couldn't. You're, like, famous." She blushed as she wrote my name on the cup, and passed it on to her colleague. I swiped my card and added a tip.

As I received my coffee, a man behind me whispered that I probably shouldn't be drinking liquids. "Y'know, rust and all." I assured him it was fine and that I've been having my morning latte for the past twenty years without any problems.

WHEN I ARRIVED at the office, Deborah from the reception told me my appointment was already waiting in my office. Ilona was early. Most new writers are eager, hungry, ready to start.

I held out my hand to greet her. She looked at it warily before shaking it, gave me a crooked smile, and shifted on the edge of the chair in front of my desk.

"Last week, when they told me you'd be my editor, I looked you up," Ilona said.

I couldn't stop myself from rolling my eyes. This happened every time I met with a new author. And my manager wondered why I didn't like to take on new writers.

She clutched her purse. "I was really impressed with your portfolio, and I'm honored to be working together." She crossed her left leg over her right, and back again. Only then did she let go of her bag and folded her hands neatly in her lap.

My mouth went dry, and I blinked a few times. Perhaps she wasn't as prejudiced as the rest of them. "I've read your manuscript, and it touched me. It needs some polish, but . . ." I smiled. "I'm convinced we could make this a hit. You must know that I'm strict and I'll be the biggest critic to read your work. I'll invite you in once I've finished my notes so we can talk it over. I meet face to face with all my new writers to get us on the same page, no pun intended. Are you okay with that?" My boss hated my process, said it took too long, but I was his best editor. He couldn't deny that my process worked.

"Yes, but can I ask you something?" she asked, with an uncomfortable but curious look on her face. I knew what was coming. "It might be a bit personal for a first meeting, and I'm sorry if I offend you. But might I ask what it's like?" Her head tilted slightly to the right as her question left her lips.

"What's 'what' like?" I folded my sweaty hands and tried to look as if I didn't know what she was talking about.

"Well, when I looked you up on the web, I found articles about your accident and your surgeries." She started to mumble. "I was wondering . . . What's it like to be one of them?"

One of them? I swallowed hard. The question wasn't new to me, but I never got used to it. Talking about my experience, something deeply private, was uncomfortable. I looked at the family portrait on my desk; the happy faces of my kids and husband calmed me down.

Ilona followed my gaze. She smiled and asked, "Is this your family?"

I nodded.

"How long have you been married?"

I touched the frame with my finger. The photo was a few years old, and I made a mental note to replace it with a more recent one. "Ten years. Anna just turned seven."

"So that was . . . after your surgeries?" She said it like it was both a question and a statement.

"Yes, I met my husband after my accident." I couldn't help a smile, thinking back to our wedding day. It was nice not having to hide parts of my body for once. Of course, I hadn't invited anyone who would've commented on it. Even my own mother wasn't invited. It allowed me to be unapologetically me. "I gave birth to my two children and breastfed them. I do things like anyone else. I'm still me. I just see better than most people, and I can no longer break any of my bones."

"I'm sorry for bothering you with my questions. I hope you still want to work with me," she said. I only nodded, not wanting to say more. "It's just . . . I never met anyone with all the . . . I don't know, wires?"

A laugh escaped me. "I might have wires on the inside, but they're not that different from veins or nerves. Maybe I've had a bit more work done, but I'm certainly not the first. People have been receiving implants and artificial limbs long before they replaced my first joints with titanium. I am like any other person. Only with less pain than I used to have. It's not all fun though, but everyone has their own struggles."

A slight blush appeared on her face.

"Do you know anyone with a pacemaker?" I asked. It often helped them understand by making a connection to something they were familiar with.

She nodded. "My dad has one."

"You could say he is one of us too. As is a wheelchair-bound person or someone wearing glasses. Many people use technological aids to navigate daily life. Some of them are on the inside, and some are on the outside." I tucked my hair behind my ear to reveal the node on my temple. "The doctors use this to communicate with the computer inside my body, and it's the only thing you'll see on the outside. But I get more looks than someone with a walking stick."

Ilona smiled, and a twinkle appeared in her eyes. "You're right. When you explain it like that, it doesn't seem like a big deal."

"It really isn't."

"It's strange they treat you so differently and call you a cyborg. You're still human."

"Damn right I am," I said. "If it wasn't for the technology in my body, I wouldn't have been alive. Let alone be able to have children. Without that stupid news article saying I was a cyborg, making all these generalizations, no one would have known. But saying 'First Cyborg Is No Monster Of Frankenstein, But Beautiful Woman' got them the attention they wanted. They didn't even care to ask me for a comment. Not that I would've given them one."

Ilona nodded. "I tried to find your statement but couldn't find it. Didn't you talk to the press at all?"

"I didn't. By the time I was ready for the media, physically and mentally, the damage was already done. It is impossible to fight against a skewed narrative — everyone that links up to a machine is an outlier; they shouldn't exist. No one was interested in hearing my side."

"It's not too late, you know. The press might not be interested, but who cares about them?"

"Who would want to read about it now, years later? Would you?"

The woman nodded fiercely. "Yes, definitely! Hearing a story from the source is worth so much more than the second-hand nonsense from the press. Your story could even help others."

"What do you mean?" I asked.

"If society become more accepting of biotech, other patients might experience more understanding from the people around them. You already have a good support system, but not everyone does."

I tapped my pen on a legal pad. "There's this homeless person living at the subway station with a prosthetic leg," I said. "I think he hates me. Every time I see him, his sneers get worse, like I did something to him. Thinking about it now, it might be jealousy."

"Why don't you ask him? If you're going to write about your transformation, why not include other people's stories as well?"

"I doubt he'll want to talk to me."

"He could be the first person whose mind you change. And you can find out more about what's needed for a good support network. You need those stories too."

"You're pretty good at this book proposal thing."

"Well, there's a reason why I'm sitting here," Ilona said and laughed. "Let's have lunch next time we meet so we can talk business. Yours and mine."

I grinned. "Deal."

TESSA HASTJARJANTO

Tessa is a disabled biracial author from the Netherlands. They have published short stories in the Dutch comic con anthology 'Heroes' and in Skullgate Media's 'Winter Wonders' anthology, in addition to their self-published work. You can find Tessa on Twitter and Instagram.

Twitter: @Endalia

Instagram: @essa.hastjarjanto

DEPRESSION IN THE BACKSEAT
JORIS FILIPP

It was at a gas station in New Mexico, just outside Tucumcari, that my depression caught up with me. Sprawled out on a bench next to the store under the midday sun, I was watching the regular crowd: A gas station attendant wearing a cap strolled past, looking quite the cliché; two unbearably cranky kids in khakis were ushered into the store by what seemed to be their parents. On the far side of the parking lot, a handful of smoking truckers sipped coffee from plastic cups. A person with short purple hair passed on their way to the store; they wore blue jeans, a sleeveless vest with patches, and a very attractive nose ring. Intrigued, I sat up. When the door to the shop slammed shut behind them, my eyes trailed back to the parking lot.

I didn't notice the car that blocked my pick-up at first. What caught my attention, however, was the manner in which everybody else did *not* take the slightest bit of notice: The gas station attendant passed the car on his way back to the store, unabashed as the plastic box he was carrying barely missed the fender; the kids in khakis, now dripping ice-cream, trotted almost right into it, not veering from their course — and the two grown-ups followed suit. Their failure to notice the obstacle drew my consciousness like a badly concealed attempt at cheating by one of my students.

The obstruction was a purple Mini. An odd, misty purple. It sat directly in front of my monster blue Nissan. Where had it come from? I hadn't seen it pull up. It was a tiny, ridiculous bubble of a car. This one's got guts, I thought. Later I would find out just what a misconception this was. *This one's got guts. Little did I know!*

Then somebody walked right through the Mini, stopped about where the backseats were, and blended with the coachwork. I squinted. Did that just happen?!

There was a guy ... probably a guy ... standing in the Mini. Or behind it. Or underneath it. Somewhere where it was not possible to stand. There was a reddish gleam on the guy, too. I realized then that the misty purple car was actually a weirdly semi-translucent red — the purple an effect of my own pickup's blue color shimmering through.

The man looked straight at me and casually walked out of the Mini headed in my direction.

My pork pie hat lay next to me on the rough wooden bench. I had taken it off to cool the sweat gathering underneath. I was on my way to the University of New Mexico in Albuquerque to give a lecture on the reproductive habits of *acroloxus coloradensis* — hermaphrodites of course, like any other pulmonate — and had stopped at the gas station to take a break.

I took the hat from the bench and put it on. Maybe I was just suffering from hallucinations due to the sun or the long hours of driving.

The shady character walked up straight to me and grinned. "Nice hat, professor."

I glanced at him. He was a tall, lean, uptight white guy wearing a white shirt, a black tailcoat, and a black hat. I knew instantly he neither was nor ever had been a student of mine. Otherwise he would have known that I prefer being addressed by my name instead of some title. I was sure I'd never seen him before. He looked as if he'd fallen out of a bygone century, yet there was something familiar about him . . .

"May I introduce myself? — I'm your depression."

I jumped inwardly, but managed to remain still apart from a twitching in my right foot, which instinctively wanted to hit an accelerator, although there was none on the sun-baked ground, of course. It kicked a fist-sized stone a good way off onto the street. What I wanted to think was: This guy badly needs a shrink. But there was a problem. *He was right.*

Which meant that *I*, not he, was in need of a shrink.

Yes, that's right. I felt it. Couldn't have put this word, this . . . label on him myself. But when he said he was my depression, I knew it was true. Like when you realize you've found exactly what you'd been looking for although you never had been looking for it. Only the other way round.

I had a way of dealing with unwanted truths: Ignore them. I stared past the guy, fixing my eyes on the store.

"Your manners leave much to be desired, Ma'am."

First a title, then a gender. I was growing more irritated by the second.

"Are you sure you've got the right person? I mean, you definitely got my gender wrong!" I said. "I don't doubt that you're a depression, but are you absolutely certain I'm the lucky person you're looking for?"

He was not to be unnerved. His eyes pierced mine, like he could see everything I was thinking.

"Absolutely," he confirmed, producing a folded handkerchief without reaching down into his pockets. He wiped the space on the bench next to me then fluttered the tails of his much-too-hot tailcoat through the air and sat down.

I swiveled the plastic cup of coffee in my hands. Here we were, sitting side by side, depression and professor. I understood right then that this day would become more cumbersome than I had expected. I already felt my energy draining, and it bothered me.

"So, D.P., what makes you so sure I'm your target?"

"I go by Depression, professor, if you don't mind."

"Actually I do. That's not a name, but a pathological condition. I'm not going to dispute with a pathological condition, never mind that its characteristics are laid down in DSM V."

"It's personality, not characteristics." D.P. shrugged. "Anyway, suit yourself."

He didn't bother to answer my original question. I waited for my foot to start drumming on the dusty ground the way it does when I'm bothered, but my foot seemed too tired to move.

"Which pronoun do you use, D.P.?" I asked aggressively, only half-caring because what I really wanted was to annoy him with the name I had chosen for him.

"He."

That being settled, my mind started to wander. I was not going to have this clown monkey around with me. I had to fill up the car, after all. And I should get the oil checked at some point. And refill the coolant. I really mustn't forget to fill up the car. Who could tell when I'd come across the next gas station? And I had to get the oil checked. Not that there was any urgency to doing it again, I'd done it when I stopped just outside Tulsa. But you never know. And then — "Hey, what's going on? What are you doing?"

"Why? What?" His voice emulated innocence in full bloom. Like a student caught plagiarizing. He was bad at it, too, but at least he didn't start crying.

I turned to him. "Listen, don't try to brain-fuck me, you hear me? You're doing some repetition thing with my thoughts, and I don't like it!"

"Professor, watch your language!"

"I don't give a shit!" My verbal outburst drained my energy. That, too, was new to me. I'd been known to make a wolf-whistling ruffian blush at the force of my curses. And now I was exhausted by *language*.

It was intolerable. I mustered all the strength I could from the anger and hurled the plastic cup towards a trash can. It hit the rim and tumbled onto the dusty pavement. Cursing, I snatched the cup from the ground and dumped it into the can. I made a few steps in the direction of my pick-up, passing the weird semi-transparent red Mini and gawking incredulously at the gravel ground shimmering through the coachwork. I had to be dreaming. I stretched out my hand to feel the car body, and it felt quite material. Normal, in fact. I wiped sweat from my brow, walked past the Mini, opened the door to my pick-up and flung myself onto the driver's seat.

I couldn't pull the door shut. D.P. was blocking it with his skinny body.

"Damn it!" I hadn't even seen him get up from the bench. "Fuck off! Now!" I shouted.

He didn't budge, but stood grinning — not at me, but towards his Mini Cooper.

I waved him away. "Get going!"

Without turning his head from his car, D.P. said, "Professor, having to make amends for your rather questionable manners might be a challenge."

I stared at him. Then I stared out the windshield. The beautiful person with purple hair was walking back from the gas station, a soft drink in hand. Wanting them to see my face, I removed my pork pie hat and leaned forward, my arm resting on the steering wheel.

They made eye contact, then looked away.

I kept looking. I swear I didn't move, but suddenly a horn sounded. My horn.

They looked back at me. Then, with a clarity that cut right through my open door, they shouted: "Macho!"

"I'm not a..."

"Macho dyke!"

I watched their soft drink sail through the air, block out the sun for a second, and drench my windshield with brown liquid. Next to me, D.P. gasped as soda splattered all over his shirt and tailcoat.

"Butch?" I offered somewhat meekly in an attempt at providing linguistic help to the purple-haired person, though I wasn't happy with the gender identity. They either didn't hear me or didn't care to acknowledge my helpful gesture, and I failed to realize that our conversation had ended.

As the person stooped to pick something up from the ground, I could still discern their body through the milky outline of the red Mini. D.P. squeezed his weedy body next to mine, using the soaked windshield as protection from whatever happened next.

The sound of cracking glass. I turned on the wipers to remove the sticky coke. D.P. gasped again. The windscreen of his Mini Cooper had cracked. They must have broken it with a stone. More stones pelted down on the metal roof of my truck. It took what felt like ages for me to link the clattering sound to the quick movements of the person stooping and throwing. The person on the other side of the Mini, the person who was *visible*, albeit somewhat blearily, *through* the Mini.

D.P. grabbed the steering wheel and hung on to it. "My . . . my car!"

That brought me back to the present. "Let go of my wheel!" I pounded his hand.

"But my windshield is cracked! I can't drive off like this!"

A viciously thrown stone flew over the top of the open door. D.P. leaned further into my vehicle.

Some dudes appeared between the cars and sprinted towards us. "He bothering you, Ma'am? We'll get him," they called out to the person pelting us with stones. I wasn't sure whom they meant by "him," but I didn't ask. I was more troubled by their angry yells and bloodthirsty looks. I couldn't possibly leave anyone to the mercy of these guys. "Shit! Get in, then. Get in the truck, quick!" I yelled. D.P. sprinted around the hood, yanked open the passenger door and jumped in.

I saw the person with purple hair turn towards the dudes, yelling a furious "Mind your own business!"

I started the engine with a loud roar. "You better buckle up," I shouted against the noise.

"I prefer not to," responded D.P.

I groaned at his response and hit the accelerator as I grabbed the steering wheel tightly and drove straight into the Mini Cooper. I backed up again to push the little car out of the way completely.

But there was no crinkling of metal, no crash . . . nothing. Nor had there been the need to back up. The Mini had disappeared.

I hit the gas, squealed past the mob and bumped out onto the road.

AFTER A WHILE, I checked my passenger seat. Next to me, very erect on the very edge of the sticky vinyl seat, D.P. balanced his stick-like body on his tiny ass. I swerved off the road and stopped the car on the shoulder. The back of my head bumped into the headrest.

"Look, that's enough. Just get out."

D.P.'s face was ashen. He sat immobile on the seat. "My windshield cracked!"

I sighed. "Yes, I saw that happen, and I don't care. Get out, will you?"

"That shouldn't have happened," said D.P.

"Nor should you be sitting next to me. Get moving..." My voice trailed off into the distance and took my thoughts along. This guy was draining me. This world was draining me. D-r-a-i-n-i-n-g me. It was so hard. So difficult to move. To think. Was this fog? Whatever it was, it was clogging my thoughts.

"You don't get it. That car can't be harmed by any material item."

I made a tremendous effort to understand what the hell he was trying to tell me. A cracked windscreen. That was very natural. Nothing to fret about. In fact, that was the most natural event in the string of weirdness that had just unfolded. Compare that to a car disappearing when I drove through it.

Ah! Slowly some of the particles of fog became lighter than the rest ("It dawned on me" wouldn't quite capture the slow process).

In a way, I could then understand his confusion, but I was more worried by the sudden disappearance of a whole car than by the cracked glass.

"What happened to your car?"

"The windshield cracked!"

"No, when it disappeared."

"Oh, that. It went back to the storage."

"Of course," I said, trying to sound sarcastic through my disbelief. Another thought fought its way through the fog: If I had made his car disappear, maybe I could make him disappear, too.

I tried very hard to think him gone, to make him disappear. I even closed my eyes trying. But when I opened them, he was still there.

He observed me carefully. "Maybe we should go for a walk? To cool down?" He sounded nervous.

"A walk?" That would take a lot of effort. I mean, I would have to open the door and move my left foot and my right foot, slide out of the car. I was exhausted already. No, I wasn't up for the physical strain. "No, I don't feel like it. Besides, I have to get to Albuquerque. What kind of music do you like? You're in charge of the radio."

I had to inhale deeply after this exhausting act of talking. No more words, please, neither from me nor from him. I didn't care whether he stayed or left — all I wanted was silence. *Why was everything so exhausting?* A walk would be too much. But we were not going for a walk. We were going to my lecture in Albuquerque. Now *that* was exhausting too. I didn't want to go to Albuquerque anymore. I didn't want to do anything. What would that look like, be like: to not to do anything? Oh, stop thinking. Just leave me alone. Everyone. The world. *Just leave me alone.* Or at least: Be quiet. Just quiet.

D.P. fiddled around at the radio, found "*Summertime Sadness.*" D.P. asked me something. I ignored it. I kept thinking about Albuquerque and how it was too exhausting to drive there and give that lecture.

It got very hot in the car. D.P. had rolled down the window. He was panting and looking at me as he fiddled around with the buttons on his tailcoat and opening and closing his mouth like a fish until I couldn't ignore him any longer.

"What?"

"Can't you go on driving? I mean, you have to go to Albuquerque, don't you?"

Yep, we were still sitting motionless on the shoulder of the highway. A touch of anger flared up inside me. "Can't you stop this heat? It's you who's responsible for it, right?"

D.P. shook his head. "Sorry, I can't."

"Then I can't drive, either. It's too exhausting."

"Let's both try, ok?"

It took inhuman effort to start the machine. A huge truck blustered up in our rear, honked his horn, and whizzed by. D.P. jumped and bumped his head into the roof, then wailed.

An automatic curse left my lips as I looked at my companion. "Hey, if you don't want to get out, then get in the back seat at least."

"What?"

"I want you as far away from me as possible," I said. "Besides, it's probably much safer to have a depression in the back seat than right next to the wheel, don't you think?"

Eyeing me suspiciously, my companion nodded once. Then he laboriously climbed behind the passenger's seat and waded through an ocean of trash before plopping onto the back seat.

A soothing voice on the radio was about to convince me that the morbid dreams I'd been having had also been the best dreams I had ever had, but I managed to turn it off.

It felt weird to have D.P. in the back of the car. It felt lonely.

I castigated myself mentally for that thought. He was messing around with my brain again, I reasoned, but I couldn't go along with the thoughts, with the loneliness. My job kept me too busy to really get to know anybody well. I pictured myself as a lonely old queer with a straw hat, sitting alone with a fishing rod in their gnarled hands, on a wooden peer, in front of a dilapidated old hut that fell apart because there wasn't anybody besides myself to keep it clean and well-kept.

But I wasn't really worth the well-kept hut. I would die in it, and they wouldn't find my body until the stench alerted some neighbors living far away. I disliked thinking about the stench. I began to imagine my dead body rotting away quickly somewhere in the desert underneath the pitiless New Mexico sun. That thought soothed me. Then I tried to imagine my funeral and the speeches given there, only to realize that I was convinced not a single mourner would show up, so there wouldn't be anybody to give any speeches.

"Professor," D.P.'s voice rasped. I noticed he was leaning forward on his seat, bringing his face closer to mine. "Professor, I don't want to cause any inconvenience, but I urge you to start the machine. It's not so hot anymore — in case you haven't noticed. We can't sit here forever. I need to go to Albuquerque."

I started the motor and listened to it roaring. "Why do you have to go to Albuquerque?" I asked.

"I can't go home. My car has disappeared. So I need to reach the next gateway. I know there is one at a gas station in Albuquerque."

"The gateway!" I loved reading science fiction. At least I had loved it up to the moment I met D.P., although I couldn't quite remember *why* I had loved it, and what exactly I meant by the thought, and what it actually felt like to love anything at all — especially the love of doing something. So I stuck to the real.

"There are lots of gas stations in Albuquerque. Which one do you need?"

"What's that?" he asked absent-mindedly.

"Which gas station —"

"Professor, we need to leave. *Now*."

"What's that?"

"Now!" His scream prompted me to look through the

windshield. Something dark, gigantic moved in the distance. It was very high, and of course, it was coming our way.

I turned off the engine and applied the handbrake firmly.

"What are you doing? Go! Go!" he screamed in anguish.

"Too dangerous to drive in a dust storm!" I replied.

D.P. didn't respond. I looked him over in the rearview mirror as the dust storm hit, shaking the car with its fury of sand and debris. It lasted for only a few minutes. When visibility returned, D.P. was still shaking.

I started the motor once again and swiveled back onto the road. For the first time since meeting my depression, my mind felt washed clean and somewhat calm.

Considering who my companion was, it shouldn't have come as a surprise that we hit diluvial rain a mere and bizarre 20 minutes after the dust storm, had a burst tire, and found a patch of mold in my lunch bag where my sandwich should have been. But I wasn't hungry anyway. I was surprised at the fact that my depression, which (who?) was sitting in the back seat, still looked shaken with fear even after I took a short pee break and returned to the car.

I had to ask him twice what was up. He mumbled something about somebody having passed us and having seen him sitting in the car, when this somebody should not have been able to see anything (anybody?) at all. Even if this somebody had checked very thoroughly, he should only have seen a small depression in the car seat upholstery (I snorted), but nothing else, and nobody would get as close to the car as to notice that. I was unempathetic; after all, I saw him too.

"As did the dudes at the gas station, didn't they?"

But D.P. shook his head. "No; they were after you, not me . . . I think."

"You mean to say they didn't see you? Then why the hell did I take you along? There was no need to! I could have left you there — invisible as you were to them, you weren't at risk!"

"I can't be certain anymore," D.P. said. "I can't be certain whether they saw me or not! All I know is that they shouldn't have!" He fell into a glum silence.

We were approaching Albuquerque rapidly. My moment of calm was over, and my thoughts were whirling around the challenge waiting for me with a well-known rapidity once again. The thought of the lecture made my belly tighten. My mind was clogged with some sticky stuff that made it impossible to think. My feet were cold (and we only had a few miles to go to Albuquerque). My arms were cold (and we were driving under the New Mexican sun!). My hands on the wheel were shaking.

There would be the usual crowd of students at the lecture. Hyenas, all of them. They would try to impress their advisors by asking sophisticated questions, and hell! I didn't know if I'd be up to answering them! I had been one of those students myself, full of ambition. I'd managed to impress quite a lot of professors by asking other professors very sophisticated questions — professors who had not been able to answer those questions and had lost face in the process. At least that's what I had thought back then.

And the advisors . . . Vultures, all of them, who pretended to be sociable while waiting for me to die of exposure. I pictured vultures with the faces of my competitors tearing apart my carcass and wolfing down pieces of it. I would get neither a proper eulogy nor a proper funeral.

I wondered why I found these morbid thoughts so calming. Was I going crazy, thinking about death and funerals? It took three attempts to make it stop. Then I remembered how I had loved to give papers and talks in the past. The attention! The spotlight! I had thrived in it. That was the true me, wasn't it?

Not this empty paper bag of a person sitting behind the wheel pretending to be a professor?

But the true me was gone, and the paper bag was all that remained. As we drove into Albuquerque, D.P. startled me by touching my shoulder. He motioned to a gas station on the right-hand side.

D.P. thanked me for the ride, wished me a great day and stalked off. Just like that. I didn't believe he would really leave me. I mean, he was *my* depression, wasn't he? But he was gone.

I filled up the car and waited for the heaviness to lift from my shoulders. I tarried. I checked the oil again (remembering clearly that I had done it just outside Tulsa). Got back in the car. Started the engine.

I was surprised when I found myself on Campus Boulevard, parked the truck, and stepped into the warm evening sun. Couldn't believe I'd really made it. Couldn't believe I was capable of thinking infantile thoughts such as "couldn't believe that I'd really made it." I mean, I had only been driving my truck, for fuck's sake!

The lecture was due to start in 90 minutes. I sat down on a bench. I got up again and dragged myself to another bench hidden away between two buildings. I should have found the colleague who had invited me to the lecture, but I couldn't face meeting him. Communicating with him, pretending to be someone — it would cost too much energy. *Impostor*, an inner voice chided me. In order to silence it, I took out my notes to review what I was going to tell the students. Sixty minutes to go. Students would soon be assembling in front of the hall. It really was high time to find the faculty members.

A commotion erupted in front of the building. I stuck my head in my notes, paying it no heed. Then, glancing over the pages, I saw D.P. hurriedly turn a corner. I wasn't even surprised to see him. Somehow I hadn't believed he had truly disappeared. I languidly waved him over to my side.

"Hey, D.P., this way. It's always good to have a friend with you when you enter the lion's den. You're welcome to listen to my lecture."

I noticed the haunted look on his face. "What's up, mate?" I asked him.

"They saw my coat!"

I had become accustomed to him making not much sense at all, so I told him that he needed to be more precise if he wanted me to understand what was going on before I would be lost in the hidden lives of *acroloxus coloradensis*.

"Some students saw my tailcoat flutter in the wind! I have no explanation for this. It shouldn't have happened. And there was no gateway at the station."

"Funny, isn't it, when these unexpected things happen all of the sudden, don't you think?"

"Ridiculous," he lashed out. "I have been subjected to bizarre things! I was required to meet you, but since I did, strange things have been happening to me. I don't understand what's going on."

"I can relate to that," I assured him. "I've never seen you so upset before." He looked forlorn, a haunted look in his eyes. And that actually made it easier for me to master my energies. "Are you worried?" I asked him.

"Hell yeah!" he answered.

I have no idea where he caught that kind of language. "What do you intend to do now?"

"I don't have any plans."

"Do you want to keep clinging to me everywhere I go?"

"I'm uncertain about the *everywhere*," he answered, waving his hands around in desperation, "but you're the only one I know this side of the barrier, and I don't seem to be able to get back!"

"I don't know which barrier you're talking about," I said.

"Well, there are many things you don't know, professor."

A silence fell between us as I contemplated what he said. "You know I will try to get rid of you sometimes, don't you?" I asked.

D.P. looked startled. "I . . . guess," he answered. Then he smiled. "So far, you haven't really done a particularly good job at that, have you?"

"I have yet to try hard enough," I mused.

He waved his hand impatiently. "Let's get you to your lecture!"

As soon as he said the word lecture, I felt the dread of having to give it once again. But I started to walk. After a few steps I noticed he wasn't next to me. I turned round and almost stepped on his toes.

"What's that? Are you hiding?"

"They mustn't . . . they mustn't see me!"

I stared at him. "You look ridiculous in that tailcoat and everything, that's true. But you can't hide behind me! They will think you're completely nuts — and I too, with this weirdo always just behind my back. You want to keep me company, fine! But you will do so right out in the open."

"But . . ."

"No negotiation!" I walked on a few steps, then looked round for D.P. who was still rooted to the spot. "You coming?"

JORIS FILIPP

Joris Filipp works for a queer organization in Berlin, Germany. They are a teacher, coach and editor and have performed in spoken word events as well as given lectures on queer and postcolonial speculative fiction. In their writing, Joris explores some of the challenges of loss and neurodiversity.

A DAWN LESS DARK
KEVIN MACK

My demon seldom visits me at night.

It visits in the early afternoon on clear spring days. Today I'm walking across a parking lot and the temperature is just right and there's only a hint of a breeze. Just like eastern Afghanistan in May. I have to take my headphones off, because if I don't, I won't hear the incoming-fire alarm when the base gets attacked. And if I don't hear the alarm, I can't take cover the way they taught us to. If we get hit, I'm vulnerable.

I pause.

But there won't be an attack, because I'm in Phoenix, and Afghanistan was ten years ago.

The demon is there, watching. The sun is high and the shadows are short, but I can see it — a shadow within a shadow, waiting for me to slip up. It's been ten years. I've kept it at bay the same way I survived in Afghanistan: with relentless tenacity and a strict adherence to discipline.

I live by a set of rules. They keep me safe. Never keep more than a six-pack in the fridge. No guns in the house. No pills.

The only exception is the Tylenol I keep for the chronic pain that came from too many ruck-marches. I'll never forget what a medic told me in Afghanistan. If you try to do it with Tylenol, they'll get you to the hospital before you die. But not before your liver fails. Then, if you don't get a transplant, it happens anyway, after two weeks of agony. And you won't get a transplant that fast.

I knew that. I never forgot it. And I believed the threat of terminal liver failure would keep me from trying. But the other night, I didn't care. The panic attacks had been happening more frequently, and the demon was there each time. I stood at the sink with the open bottle in my hand. I was ready. I didn't care. But then the demon appeared. It must've thought it finally had me, but my hand shook so badly I dropped the bottle into the sink and cowered in the corner until it got bored and left.

Tonight I'm going to exorcise my demon permanently. I've been researching on the internet. I've gathered everything I need; I've even got a spot picked out, and tonight I'm going to be free.

THE FIRST THING you need if you're going to exorcise a demon is its name.

You have to summon it in order to bind it. One way to summon a demon is to call it by name. Once it's bound, you can cast it out, but you must start with the summoning. It knows this. Which is why it's never going to let you learn its name.

But there's a loophole.

You can summon a demon by giving it an enticing environment. That doesn't mean some barren hell-scape, by the way. It could be a recreation of the circumstances where it's prone to visit you.

Which is why I'm driving out to the middle of the desert after midnight. I made a habitat for my demon. I park my truck about fifty yards away. It's a flat little spot above the bank of a dried-up creek. They call creek beds 'wadis' in Afghanistan, whether they say it in Arabic, Pashto, or Urdu. I figure if it reminds me of that place, it'll work for calling up the demon, too.

My overriding memory of Afghanistan was the number of stars you could see — in the middle of nowhere, there weren't any man-made lights. And tonight is perfect. Clear and cold and I can just make out the Milky Way.

Tonight is so clear that I can't distinguish Orion. He's usually really easy to spot — the three bright stars make up his belt. But the sky is so cluttered with stars you never get to see, that it takes several minutes to find them: Alnitak, Alnilam, and Mintaka. Most stars have Greek names, but these are Arabic. That's my trigger. I hear something in Arabic, or I see a Quranic ceremony, and I'm back in the war.

See, I wasn't an Islamophobe before I ran to the recruiter's office the day after 9/11. I don't think I am now, either, but I can't tell. Yeah, I know "Islamic" and "Arabic" aren't the same thing, but if you put two next to each other and stare at them long enough, they blur together. It happened to a lot of us over there. The enemy always shot rockets after morning azaan — that's the call to prayer that the chanter shouts from the minaret. And since the minaret overlooked the base, I'd wake up when I heard the chanting. Then a few minutes later, "Incoming! Incoming! Incoming!" in that robotic voice accompanied by the siren.

It doesn't matter if it's the azaan, or war movies, or three stars with Arabic names. I have triggers. It's pure Pavlovian conditioning. Stimulus and response: I hear a word in Arabic, and the rage comes back. I don't want to hate anymore. Hate was how I survived the war. And now it's what feeds the demon, and I want them both gone.

I step out of the truck. It's cold, and it's clear, and there's the Milky Way. I feel the same way I did over there, even though I know I'm not, and the demon comes creeping. But I sense it, at the edge of my vision, just past the range of my flashlight.

I breathe in, breathe out, put my hand on the fender. Then I shine the light on the driver's front wheel, count the lug nuts. I push the demon away, but not so far that it's all the way gone — I need it to come back when I'm ready to bind it.

Don't summon a demon if you aren't absolutely sure you can bind it.

Remember when I said I had a spot picked out? I've been pulling up sagebrush and Russian thistle and prickly pears over the last few weekends. I tried to run off all the wildlife I could find. It's too cold for snakes and there weren't many rabbit holes. Just lizards and scorpions.

I drive a tent stake into the center of the clearing. I need to trace a series of five concentric circles, at ten-foot increments. I measure and cut my rope lengths: fifty, forty, thirty, twenty, ten feet. I tie a rope to the stake and use it to form a radius and pour salt from the canisters I brought. If I keep the rope taut as I walk around the stake, it forms a circle. Demons like concentricity. I'm not sure why.

The circles represent the five classical elements. I place an object within each of them. Five circles, five objects.

For the outermost circle, air. A toy Blackhawk helicopter, like the one of the thousands we sent to the war. I check the batteries, then turn it on. The rotor blades spin with an electric whine, and it kicks up a little dust from years of seeing the inside of an old box.

Next, water. I choose a cup of hot chai tea. All those 'advisors' we sent overseas, winning hearts and minds — for all the good it did when we pulled out — drank chai with the tribal leaders, made deals, bought promises. Some we reneged on, some they did.

Third, earth. My boots. I've worn the soles flat; they're more black than tan. Grease, hydraulic fluid, who knows what else. It wouldn't surprise me if there was still some Afghan dirt ground into the leather.

Fourth, fire. I brought road flares. We always carried flares with us in the desert. Signaling friendly positions, showing an aircraft where to land. A flare is simply burning metal. Have you ever seen an armored vehicle or an airplane catch fire? I have. Guess where.

Then there's the fifth element. Soul, spirit, life . . . *blood*. In the movies, they feign cutting the inside of their palm. Do it that way in real life, you'll regret it for the next week. Instead, I drag my blade across my forearm. It doesn't bleed much. I'm not sure if that's good or bad. I don't go deeper, though. Once, I saw a lance corporal who got hit by shrapnel. Severed some of those forearm tendons. The docs said she'd never be able to splay her fingers again. I'll just wait for the blood to collect and drip into the center of the circles.

Don't use wits to fight a battle of wills.

Once you've summoned and bound a demon, convincing it to stay away is pretty easy. According to the Internet, anyway. They don't like to be trapped, so you just have to hold out long enough to get it to surrender. Demons have to adhere to the terms of their deal. So I've heard. But don't let the demon dictate the terms.

I take a deep breath and begin.

"Demon, I summon thee."

I don't want to admit I'm expecting the wind to pick up, but I am. It doesn't. The air of the empty parking lot is as still and suffocating as the demon's ever-present hold on my mind.

"Demon, heed my call."

Okay, look. I want a wolf to howl or something. I know we don't have wolves around here, but a coyote could at least yelp.

"Demon, I call you forth."

It's just me and the stars and the red-white flicker of the road flare.

"Demon. Thrice by your name, I bind you. To my will thou art bound. I call you forth and bind you in this circle."

Nothing. Silence. The road flare burns out with a fizzle. Now it's just me and the darkness. I'm cold and alone. A soft breeze wanders across the desert. All those times the demon came unbeckoned and now it leaves me alone? I can't muster a reaction. My shoulders slump under the weight of desperation and defeat.

Then I see it. Except it isn't an 'it.'

It's a them.

Three vague figures stand at the edge of the outermost

circle. I can't tell what I'm looking at because the flare messed up my night vision, but I can see them advance towards me.

I stand my ground. This is part of the plan. They have to reach the center of the circles. The five elemental objects should've enticed them.

Maybe I've read too much urban fantasy, but I expect something to happen as they cross each line of salt — a shimmer or a flash of light or something. Yet they're just walking as if the salt does nothing.

I feel a chill, but not a real chill. It's that nervous feeling telling me to be careful. As if I needed the reminder. They've crossed the third line now. I got to my feet. Their demonic compulsions drive them inward. Once they cross the fifth circle, they'll be fully bound. I've got to hold out for at least that long.

They are close enough now I can tell them apart. One is feminine. Two are masculine. All are wearing military uniforms of some form or another. They don't look diabolical. I don't know what I was expecting — horns or whatever — but they look like soldiers.

I've held out as long as I can. They enter the center circle and I run. I pace my strides to leap over the lines. If I break a salt line, they'll be free to pursue me. When I'm sure I've cleared the last circle, I turn to look.

They are following me. Their stride is steady and relentless, inexorable.

Perhaps the binding wasn't strong enough, or they combined their strength to overcome me.

Less than a hundred feet now to the truck. I hear the crunch of gravel under their boots, closer and closer.

I STAGGER and scrabble at the ground. I fumble in my pocket for the key fob. I press the unlock button again and again until the running lights are blinking like the muzzle flash of an automatic rifle.

The last few scrambling steps get me to the door. I climb into the driver's seat and slam the door. I jab the key in the ignition, but I miss. I try again, hands shaking. The key scrapes against the bezel. I jam it and try to force it. I make myself slow down, steady my hand, and feel it slide into the ignition. A silent cheer erupts inside me until I notice something at the edge of my vision.

A demon sits in the passenger seat.

My hand reaches for the handle and the door locks of its own volition — or the demon's. I turn and brace myself against the door, my feet on the bench seat between me and whatever is in the truck. I'm ready to make a stand, my last stand, if that be the case. Then I get a good look at it. It's the feminine one and —

I recognize her. Fear gives way to confusion, then nausea. It takes a hard swallow to settle my stomach.

"Why do you look like Katie?" I ask.

"Because, I am Katie," she says.

"No. You're a demon. Why aren't you trapped in the circle?"

"I'm not a demon. I'm Katie."

"What, like a ghost?"

"Sure, if that makes this easier for you. How do you think I got in here without opening the door?"

Okay, fair point. I allow myself a moment to assess the situation. She's sitting in the passenger seat, hands folded in her lap. Her uniform is the old-style digital camo pattern that got phased out a few years ago. It was the regulation pattern when Katie and I served in Afghanistan. She's rolled her sleeves up to her biceps, revealing her tattoo, the traditional Samoan malu she started, but never got to finish. Katie hasn't got a helmet on, and her dark hair is in that too-tight bun long-haired women had to wear before the military changed the regulations. She's wearing body armor, though, and she's got a pistol in a drop-leg holster around her thigh.

"Shouldn't you be glowing, or see-through, or something?"

"It doesn't really work like that."

"Why are you here?"

"You summoned me, didn't you?"

"No. I summoned the demon that's been following me for the last ten years. Is it you? Have you and your buddies out there," I motion to the other two spirits standing motionless outside the truck, "been doing this to me?"

"No. I — we — have been trying to help you. We come to you when you need us, but you keep pushing us away."

"Pushing you away? You are forcing me to relive the worst moments of my life! I can barely hold a job. I've scared away all of my friends, the ones who are still alive, anyway. How is that supposed to help me?"

"Let me show you."

She reaches a hand towards mine. I flinch and pull my hand away, but her palm brushes over the back of my hand. Soft. Too soft to be that of a ghost.

When I look up, I'm sitting in the back of a Humvee.

From what I can guess by the lack of shadows outside, it's close to midday. We're on a dirt road, and everything is brown and tan. The glare of the sunlight hurts my eyes, even through the ugly wraparound sunglasses I'm now wearing. Katie is still sitting next to me, only now her helmet is on and she's got ugly sunglasses too.

I know where we are, and I know what's about to happen, but I've got to ask, anyway.

"Is this what I think it is?"

Before she can answer, the air around me compresses into a tangible wall. I feel, rather than hear, the explosion. In less than the sweep of a second hand, it strikes my entire body; the air forced out of my lungs. I gasp, lungs burning, then grab the seat-back as the vehicle whips through the air.

The Humvee rolls several times, then slides to a stop on its roof. Katie is hanging in her seatbelt, unmoving. I claw my way across the bench seat to check on her, but I can't make it. It's as if some unseen force is holding me in place, not my fear, but a presence that demands I bear witness. I hear shouts of "Allahu akbar!" and the sound of sporadic gunfire.

Katie's eyes open. She tries the latch on her buckle. It doesn't release. She tugs frantically, yanking at the straps, which won't budge. I shout, but she doesn't acknowledge me. She pulls a knife from her vest and slices at the straps. She makes progress, cutting herself along the way. Her blood spreads across her shoulders and thighs, drips onto the ceiling.

Then she's free. Her hand shoots up, down really, as she falls. Her head strikes the roof of the vehicle, the weight of her body collapses onto her neck. And it bends at an impossible angle.

The next moment we're at Katie's funeral. Her parents are there — another family grieving another senseless loss. Her little brothers stand next to her parents. I never met them, yet I know they looked up at her. Their eyes are red and tearful, but they've set their jaws and furrowed their brows in hard pride. She was their hero, and they can't comprehend that she's gone. That's not what happens to heroes.

Her sister is a different story. I know that look. Expressionless, but swollen — puffy and red. The eyes are hard, rigid. The muscles bulge at the corner of her jaw. I wonder what words went unspoken between the sisters.

I'm back in the truck. Katie still sits in the passenger seat, eyes straight ahead. I don't know what to say to her.

"My sister thought she could beat this on her own. She can't. Neither can you."

She leads me back to the circles. I can see the other two figures better now, one in a flight suit, the other in camouflage fatigues. The latter approaches me. He wears a beard and has an Afghan flag on his uniform.

His uniform is special forces, Namir — tigers.

I never liked working with Afghan special forces. The Taliban sent infiltrators to join them, then when they partnered with our forces, they'd go on a rampage and kill as many of us as they could before we stopped them.

Namir turns to me. "As-Salamu 'alaikum," — peace be upon you in Arabic.

I'm supposed to say "wa-'Alaikum as-salaam," — and upon you peace — but I don't. I can't tell the good ones from the bad.

Namir puts out his hands to grab me by the shoulders and give me a kiss on the cheek, so I put my fists up to stop him. He grabs my shoulders anyway, and when he does, we're in another time and place. Just like with Katie.

This time it's a different Humvee. The back half is obliterated, smoke pouring from the wreckage and debris flung out in the blast pattern of a roadside bombing. Namir braces his rifle on the hood of the vehicle. There's a ridge on the other side. Namir is firing towards it. Other Afghans, along with American Special Forces, are fighting together. There are a myriad of muzzle flashes coming from the ridge — enemy fighters incoming. It's a battle I've seen before. Maybe not this exact battle, but the textbook roadside ambush that characterized the entire war.

"Allahu akbar!" Namir shouts.

I freeze. That's what the bad ones say — Taliban, Al Qaida, or lone wolves, as if it made a difference whose team they were on. 'God is greater.' That's their battle cry. Like when they killed Katie. It's what that US Army Major said when he murdered those people at Fort Hood.

But when Namir says it, Afghans on both sides start saying it. They're shouting it back and forth as they try to kill each other. Namir jolts back, as a bullet strikes his upper torso. His left arm drops. With his right, he reaches into his pocket. Then he's hit again. Lower torso. Right side. That one got a lung, I'm sure. Another cripples his leg, and he collapses to the ground.

The others run from cover to cover. They fire and fight, but no one can stop to help. I run to him and kneel, but as with Katie, I am bound to watch. I can't intervene. His breathing slows, but his eyes are open. Clear. And he speaks.

"Allahu akbar," he gasps. *God is greater.*

His respiration is speeding up, but the breaths are shallower. "Allahu akbar."

He looks just like one of our guys when they get hit. Scared. Then calm as they die.

Muhammad descended from Abraham the same as Jesus. So when Namir says "Allahu akbar," he's invoking the God of Muhammad, the God of Abraham. My God.

When our guys get hit and they keep repeating *Please, God. Don't let me die*, they've been calling out to the God of Abraham. When we take cover behind rocks or Humvees and try to kill each other, we convince ourselves we do it in the same God's name.

If we're children of the same God, then we are brothers. So, I have to ask myself what right I have to demand God's blessing as I kill His child.

I know the answer.

I would always have known the answer if I'd allowed myself to consider it. Which is why I never did. Because if I'd acknowledged that fundamental truth, I'd lose the ability to pull the trigger. That's why they were called 'haji' or 'jib' or 'Jafar.' That's why my forebears called their adversaries 'japs' or 'huns' or 'rebs.' They couldn't kill their brothers, so they made them into something less.

I look at Namir. His breathing is faint. His eyes lose focus, and the life seeps out of them. I have to stay there with him. There's a sergeant shouting into a radio. A corporal is waving a flare at a helicopter approaching the battlefield. When it lands, the medics rush to Namir. They examine him for a moment, but it's too late. They put him in a body bag and I follow them aboard. The helicopter flies to Bagram Air Base. The crew unloads the wounded, then they come for Namir. That's when I learn body bags aren't watertight. Namir's heart had stopped beating, but his blood continued to flow from the wounds along his back and leg where the bullets exited. The blood pooled in the bag, and when they drag him away, it leaves long red streaks out of the helicopter.

Even after this man has died, the stain of his death remains on me just as his blood stains the floor of the aircraft. The hot Afghan day turns to cold dark night. I shiver.

We are back inside the circles. He embraces my shoulders, kisses my cheeks. "Ma'a as-salaama." Namir bids me farewell.

I hated him for the deeds of other men. But he didn't suffer from my hate. I did.

I place my right hand to my heart and tell him "Jazakallah khair," — may God reward you with goodness.

NAMIR LEADS me to the center of the circles, to the last figure. I recognize him now, too. Slightly taller than average, slightly skinnier. Brown-haired Air Force pilot.

"Bulldog?" I ask.

He steps towards me, extends his hand. When I take it, I'm transported again. Like with Katie and Namir, I expect to relive Bulldog's death. But that's not what I see.

I see a woman, approaching forty. And a girl maybe twelve or thirteen. I recognize the woman. Bulldog's wife. I'd only met her once, not well enough to keep in touch after he died, but I'm sure it's her. And the girl wasn't even walking at the time. I doubt she has any memory of her father.

They're sitting on separate couches around a coffee table in a living room. The woman is reading; the girl is watching something on the TV. A man enters the room. It's not Bulldog. This isn't the past, it's now. The young girl perks up her head, and the woman rises to kiss him.

I feel my face flush. My blood pressure rises and my temples throb. I clench my fists and turn to Bulldog.

"Unbelievable. Everything you sacrificed for her, and this is how she thanks you," I say.

But when I turn to him, there's a contented smile on his face.

"You've got it wrong," he says. "I want them to be happy. And most of the time, they are."

"Yeah, but you got killed and everyone back home . . ." I motion to the family in the living room, "goes about their lives like nothing happened. It's not fair."

"No. It isn't. Would you feel better if they were miserable?"

"Of course not."

"Should they spend their lives wallowing in bitterness and resentment? Should they hold on to the past so tightly the present passes them by and the future never happens? Should they go through life with ghosts — demons, if you want — following them, haunting them, tormenting them?"

He's talking about me, but I can't let go of the past, the memories, the loss, and the resentment.

"Your wife and daughter knew you better than I did. And they were closer. They should be the ones thinking about you every day, not me."

Bulldog lays a hand on my shoulder. "You think they don't think about me every day? You think she didn't think about me the day she remarried? She processed it. It doesn't mean it's over, or that she's forgotten about me. But she's gotten herself to where she can move on with her life and — this is the most important part—she's gotten to a point where she can be happy again. It's time for you to do the same."

"I didn't let myself grieve for you," I confess. "A family needs to grieve more than a friend does, so it isn't fair for me to take that from them."

Bulldog lets me pace, full of nervous energy with no outlet, before he responds..

"Taking some grief for yourself doesn't steal it from someone else."

I contemplate Bulldog's death. He was flying in formation with another aircraft the night he crashed. Later, I saw the video from the second plane's infrared camera. It had audio. Bulldog's last words haunted me. *Still haunt me.* They weren't even words. He made a guttural groan, a perverse mix of fear and disgust. Thinking back on it makes me angry. Like with Katie and Namir. The pointlessness of their deaths at the whim of a disinterested politician invokes a fury that clouds out the sadness I need — and now want — to express.

A memory intrudes upon my rage. Me and Bulldog passing time in a USO lounge at a stop en route to Afghanistan. I don't remember what we were talking about, but Bulldog laughs, and smiles his carefree smile. A smile that no one will get to see again.

That's when I break.

It's my turn for guttural groaning. I'm hyperventilating and sobbing. My knees buckle and I collapse into a fetal crouch. I'm weeping and gasping. I can't stop myself from shuddering. Then there's a hand on my shoulders. And another. And another.

I don't rush myself through the experience, and neither do the others. I embrace it, finally, after so many years of running from it. After several minutes, I've cried enough and can breathe steadily. There is a void now, where before there was only grief. Oh, there is still grief. I can still feel it. But in that void, there is room for something else.

I stand to see Bulldog, Katie, and Namir. We're back in the center of the circles.

"That's what you meant when you said I had to grieve in order to move on," I say to Bulldog, but when I look up, he's gone. They're all gone. Yet I know I'm not alone. Nor can I continue alone. I have to find my brothers and sisters, the ones who can't let go. Katie's sister, the soldiers who partnered with the Afghans, Gold Star Wives like Bulldog's. I have to share my grief with them and learn from them in turn. *Our* grief will be less than my grief and theirs.

I wish I can say that's when the dawn breaks and the sun

rises on a brand new day or something suitably cheesy, but it doesn't. It's still dark. I'm not cured or recovered or anything like that. I haven't reached my destination, but now I'm ready to move and I know which way to go. I make my way back to the truck. The keys are still in the ignition. I start the truck and pull out onto the dirt road to make my way home.

And maybe the sky above the eastern horizon is a little less dark.

KEVIN MACK

Kevin Mack is a disabled combat veteran who spent a decade flying rescue helicopters in the US Air Force. When not writing, he can be found hiking the American Southwest with his family. Find Kevin on Twitter.

Twitter: @KevinCMack

WHAT REMAINS
ALLISON BAGGOTT-ROWE M.A.

The corpse had been sitting there for three minutes and forty-four seconds when he realized he was not breathing. The newspaper lay idly open to page six of the Sports section, more than halfway through a story covering the Mariners' current hot streak cut short by the visiting team in the top of the 6th inning. What a shame; they had really gotten into a rhythm in the past month or so.

A spider, suspended over the shade of his antique reading lamp, was staring at him from the corner of the room, quivering on a singular length of silken thread. The picture of a young Japanese-American girl was perched askew in a cheap, plastic frame with no glass. The lamp hummed in an otherwise darkened one-bedroom apartment at the corner of Mulberry and Vine. Even now in the early dusk, sounds of children laughing on bicycles drifted in through the east window where the A/C unit was propped up between the pane of glass and the sill. It was a scorcher of a summer day. Or perhaps, *it had been* a scorcher of a summer day.

The sounds of mothers calling their children in for dinner

were a distant memory as porch lights flickered on. Almost every house had the faint blue light of a TV screen emanating from some front-facing window. The neighborhood where the corpse had grown up, had raised his own family, was going to bed.

As he made the startling discovery that he had stopped breathing, the corpse did what any self-respecting, sentient thing would do in some such embarrassing occurrence. Staring straight ahead, he focused all his attention on his nose and mouth and sucked the stale room air through his cracked lips. To his horror, it sounded like one solitary hiccup and felt like the first time he had tried swimming underwater and had come up choking on chlorine. This tasted worse. The oxygen and nitrogen danced deliriously around his chest cavity for a moment before he burped them out.

He was dumbfounded. How had this happened to him, of all people? Right under his very nose while he was sitting in his armchair reading the Sports page. What would people think? This was a respectable neighborhood where respectable families grew up. He had no business interrupting that, no matter what hour of the day it happened to be.

Hoping that perhaps he was just having a spell of one of those mental illnesses he heard about on the segment during NPR's "Wait, Wait, Don't Tell Me," he held two fingers to his jugular and felt for a pulse. Not so much as a flutter. Goodness, at a time like this he could not even do himself the courtesy of having a pulse. How long had the host said a body could last without oxygen? He cast his mind back, but simply could not remember.

He could call his daughter, but he did not want to worry her with his problems.

He knew what finding a corpse could do to someone.

Perhaps he could call 911, but that would be quite the story to explain to the operator. It also seemed as though they might be a touch too late to really help. He blinked, which consisted of closing his eyelids over the hardening marbles in his eye sockets one at a time and then peeling them back again, feeling an unnatural stickiness that would have made a still-working stomach sour. Refusing to ruminate on the sensation, he ticked his eyes down to look at his too-white knuckles curled over the paragraph detailing the 8-3 loss. His fingertips were the softest shade of an actual cerulean sea mariner's scales. He opened and closed his fist a few times, feeling the futile crackle that said, "It is too late."

Repressing the itchy rubbing of synapses in his amygdala — "Wait, Wait, Don't Tell Me," had just been talking about where "fear" came from — he allowed his hardening arteries to continue shutting off the mainframe to the right chamber of his heart. His thoughts buzzed with the static of not enough electricity as the image of his daughter's face swam in front of his own. The last time he had seen Airi, she had been wearing her mother's fringe jacket. His wife's jacket.

He shuddered with the recollection and felt his knee collide with the folding tray table in front of him. He was mercifully unaware of his pinky toe beginning the long process of falling off as the table jarred his whole leg.

Sitting in the old armchair with the cushion that supported his back just so, the corpse ran one of his still-warm hands over his salt and pepper hair. With practiced effort, he forced his mind away from his daughter and wife. Now was not the time for thinking; it was too late and would just be a waste of time. Perhaps, though, he still had a little time left for action. His thoughts chased each other around his slowly decaying brain in a tumbling mess that reminded him of watching his clothes go around and around at the laundromat. He rose, knees protesting, and shuffled into the half-bath down the hall. Switching on the fluorescent light, he looked himself over in the mirror.

It wasn't so bad, not really. He had celebrated his 78th birthday last month with Airi. She had come over to his apartment with a Costco cake and everything. They had watched Jackie Chan movies just like old times. Of course, she had left by 8 p.m. to be back in the city before it was too late. He had not asked what she might be late for, leaving like that. She was being kind with the little white lie to make him feel better as they no longer had anything to talk about since her mother died. And watching Jackie Chan was just fine with him.

Now, in the harsh bathroom lighting he could see the liver spots on his arms that the arnica bruise cream just could not combat. The bags under his eyes had deflated like old mylar balloons, remnants of the nights when he would fell asleep in his armchair in front of the ballgame sometime around the fifth inning, waking up to a highlights reel of the game many hours later. The skin on his face was pale, had always been pale, but was now pasty white. Even his lips were white; that was new.

Better than full on rigor mortis blue, he thought idly, switching the light back off and shuffling back to his chair in his house slippers.

When would rigor mortis set in anyway? Did he have to stay still for that to happen? God, how much more did he have to do to coax his body to just rest?

He had never been good at resting. Even before his wife died, he had always struggled to go to bed at the same time she did. He had tried, God help him, but some people were just wired differently. He would close his eyes and picture her evening robe with its faded pink and purple flowers. The way the cotton bunched at the waist with the sash she would tie after her evening shower.

"I'm tired," Yurei would say to him.

"Don't you want to see Ichiro? He's on deck," he would respond half-heartedly, already turning the TV volume down.

She would not respond, tidying up her teacup and saucer before making towards the hallway that led to the bedroom. She would switch off the hall light once she reached the bedroom and call back to him in flawless Japanese, "I'm going to bed."

"Be there in a minute," he would mumble blearily, half-roused from the stupor in his chair. But it would be several hours before he woke up enough to go to bed. To prop himself up and shuffle his aching knees toward the bedroom only to discover the light was still on. To see the pink and purple flowers thrown haphazardly on the floor only to realize that two pale blue feet poked out from underneath. He fell on his creaking knees next to her and pulled her limp, lifeless body into his arms, her patiently-combed black hair still covering her face. When he had the courage to turn her over, he saw her eyes frozen wide with shock and blurred emptiness and instantly wished he had not.

His eyes flew open.

He was still in the living room, in his chair, the newspaper open to page six of the Sports section. It could have been the very same night when he should have, for once, gone to bed when she did. Maybe if he had found her in time . . . but now, here he was, a corpse himself, and he didn't know the first thing to do.

Had she wandered out of the bedroom and gone to look at her reflection in the bathroom mirror? Had she considered kindly coming out into the living room to inform him of her untimely demise so that he might do something about it?

No; she had not. Of course not. What a ridiculous thought.

Maybe this is just how it is for some people before they die, he mused. Well, he had died, but he hadn't really *died* died yet.

With a twinge that would have felt like palpitations to a living person, the corpse looked outside at the inky black night sky. He had done his time placating a religious and superstitious wife by making offerings to the kami to keep evil spirits out of his family's house. He had offered up the optimistic prayers of a faith that she espoused would bring him to Oneness with the universe when his body failed.

He flexed his hand, the skin going taut and rubbery over the arthritic knuckles with none of the usual blue veins rising to the surface like rivers on a well-read map. It was just pale, still faintly pink, and soft around the wrist if you were really looking for color. He was.

The corpse was getting angry now. Had his body failed? Or had his mind? He looked from white-pink wrist to black sky and back again. There was no Oneness. Where had all his prayers gone, anyway?

And then with a gulp. *Where would he go?*

Did he really have to wait in this body for his funeral rites to take him onward to ... well, whatever came next?

He thought he had known.

Clenching a fistful of hair, he closed his eyes and would have cried if his tear ducts had not shut down fifteen minutes ago. He thought back to the week after his wife had died. Yurei's reikon rites had been set for a week after he found her in the bedroom Long enough to call his daughter in Europe and fly her home to their small suburb of Seattle. Long enough to pay for plane tickets to bring in the family from mainland Japan, who had been so angry at his bringing young, pregnant Yurei to the states that none of her brothers came to honor her in death.

Only Airi came from out of town on that sweltering August

day. Her dark, jet black hair so much like her mother's, swept up into a style that screamed *vogue* or *couture* or some other high-fashion words his American tongue could not wrap around even on days not dedicated to mourning. She came wearing a sharp yet somber outfit she would later tell him was a woman's name, like you could wear a person.

Maybe she knew things he did not.

The service was nice, neighbors would tell him in the days to come. *Your wife would be proud of the daughter you have raised.*

Airi had decided to stay in town for a while. She called it "extending her visit" but he knew she was lying to him. She got the same look on her face that Yurei did when he would ask her if the Sounders had won their game, and she would laugh with that non-committal smile on her face that let him know she still was not picking up English.

Over dinner, he would ask Yurei if she was happy enough in Seattle, raising their daughter in the neighborhood he had grown up in. He would ask her if meeting in university and spending two semesters in her native country on study abroad had really been enough time for her to make the decision to keep the baby. If she really would rather bear the dishonor of having his mixed-race baby here in America as his wife rather than merely a tainted reputation in her home country. She would laugh with that smile and go back to eating her rice one grain at a time and rock the baby with her lily-white foot.

This was a punishment, the corpse thought, for the shame they both would carry for going through with it all.

"What do you mean, you're bringing a girl home?" the corpse's father had asked over the crackling of the long-distance call more than 50 years ago. Bringing a girl home had been the least of it. Bringing a *pregnant, unmarried* girl home had been the final nail in the coffin for summoning the corpse into the family business to pay for his illiterate bride-to-be and the fetus they had made by mistake. A disgrace.

Airi, the once-fetus, extended her trip several times until she finally decided she would be one of those progressive women who work-from-home, never mind what her office might think. He was not really sure what she did, truth be told. It sure seemed like it was more than enough to pay the bills and live in one of the many bustling metropolis satellites built for young families.

And Airi made sure everyone knew she did not want to start a family.

She moved into Seattle proper after her mother died, investing in a shoebox of an apartment she stuffed full of cats so he could not possibly go visit. It was a matter of his allergies. He made sure everyone knew that. She visited him regularly the first year, anyway, and then every month or so the year after that until she would just come over and pop in the Jackie Chan films from her childhood that had made her mother laugh. Eventually she began just sending him a check every month as he took fewer and fewer cases at his law firm.

"Just a little something as a thank you from your daughter," she would say.

But he knew better. He wished he could give the money back, but she would just write another check for more. And his smaller-than-anticipated pension had not stretched nearly as far as he had planned. He had been in the process of considering what it would mean to downsize to an apartment in the same neighborhood. Since Yurei was gone, it was just a matter of donating the things he did not need and moving out of the two-story brick house he had bought with his first year's earnings from the law firm for his wife and one-year-old daughter. He pretended he did not know Airi had rescued and put most of the items up for resale and added the value to those infuriating checks.

When neighbors saw the FOR SALE sign pitched at an odd angle in the lawn of the brick two-story, he waved off the fearful, furrowed brows and worried wrinkles that plagued the familiar faces.

"My daughter just moved back," he had said. "It would be frivolous to hang onto the house at this point." He would lower his voice to a hushed, reverent tone as if they each were in on the secret. "It's just too much, you know. Since her mother *died*."

Jolted out of his reverie with the sound of the cuckoo clock, the corpse watched the second hand tick around and wondered how much time he had left. How long until someone discovered him here? He opened his eyes and looked down at his flannel pajama bottoms. Did he really want to be found in this?

Not that it was his choice, but really, what would his old partners at the firm think? He could see the headline on the paper tomorrow:

"Corpse Found in His Pajamas: A Scandal"

Yurei had known to wear her silk house robe, he thought petulantly. The flowers on the robe had carpeted her body in what the corpse had thought might be a preview of the abundance in the afterlife. Was he even going to get to that part?

For a fraction of a second, he imagined one of the boys from work coming in to check on him after enough missed calls. Surely someone would notice when he wasn't there at the normal time tomorrow.

It was true that he wasn't putting in the same number of hours he used to with Petersen & Petersen. He would be the first to admit it, and proudly, even, if not completely honestly. Early retirement had never been a part of the game plan.

But that's how it goes if you play the game, he thought bitterly. You never know what kind of pitch you'll be swinging at when you get to the plate. All you can do is step up and take your swing.

He had that corner office for the better part of two decades before the "promotion" to a cushy back office. He had the luxury of a personal assistant to "prioritize" the company cases, slowly giving him fewer and fewer until there were days he found himself occupying his time waiting for the lunch order to make its way around the office before volunteering to set out and pick it up. Not that his personal assistant would ever let that happen, but boy did he have a sense of humor for suggesting he might run an errand.

The invitations to office parties had thinned as much as his caseload when the partners approached him for a mid-afternoon meeting to go through the particulars of his tenure with the firm. He had contributed quite a lot; many burgeoning case managers had been hired to take on the wealth of clients he had attracted over the years. It was just that, well, he had reached his — what did they call it? Had they gone so far as to call it prime? Golden years?

He couldn't remember now and it was probably best that way. In any case, he just didn't quite "have it" the way he used to. He could stay in the back office, of course, to keep up appearances. After all, it had been his father's and his brother's business before he had ever stepped foot inside the building, and twenty years of work should buy something, if not the robust retirement fund he had planned on having. It wasn't that he had overstayed his welcome, exactly, he just wasn't the first face clients needed to see these days. He could understand that in the grand scheme for what was best in the company's interest, couldn't he?

Almost involuntarily, he shook his stiffening neck as he

remembered nodding along, holding onto the fact that he could retain the keys to this office. The office he had used for his father when he had kindly phased him out during his first few years at the firm. It had been time, really, and it was best to keep that sort of thing in the family. It was the circle of life and who was he to fight it?

Heaving something akin to a sigh, the corpse supposed that everyone had to be found, one way or another. He supposed also it didn't really make sense on a Sunday evening for him to be unwinding at home in a suit, although he would have preferred for people to remember him that way. If only he had continued moving around his S&P 500 stocks for a few extra hours after dinner, he wouldn't even be in this awkward situation. Now he had to completely reconstruct what a regular night looked like for him. There just weren't that many stocks to move around at this point with how much disposable capital he had. It wasn't like he could just liquidate everything on a whim. Or maybe it *was* exactly like that.

"Take the money, Yurei," he had said in a broken attempt at Japanese. A full year had not been enough to help him completely master the language, even living entrenched in the culture every day. Then he had to pack everything he had brought on study abroad into his backpack and call her from the pay phone around the corner by the sashimi place where they had met just a few months ago.

Traffic roared around them as the rain fell on the bus station roof. Yurei had shaken her head, pulling the woolen sweater closer to cover her mouth with tears running in rivulets down her almond-shaped face.

"We don't have the money for a baby, Yurei," he lowered his voice and at the same time pushed his hand out flat to pin the cash against her stomach, which was just starting to round with the hardness of a decision already made. Raindrops landed on the hundreds he had pulled out of his checking account this morning. It was all he had, but taking care of this sort of thing was expensive. How could Yurei not see that?

His father would never need to know. Plans would go on exactly as they had expected as soon as he got home. In fact, when he had called not two hours ago, letting his father know he was cutting his trip short to get started with the company, he thought he might have even detected a hint of pride in his father's voice. He never needed to know about what had really happened in Japan. About Yurei and her...condition.

She had looked down at his hand full of American dollars clawing into the sweater covering her belly. His fingers were free of the blue map and wrinkles of experience that he would recall in vivid detail after she died. Yurei had closed her eyes before wiping them dry with her left sleeve. She slowly lowered her small hand on top of his with all the weight of a butterfly landing on a flower petal. She had risked a glance up at him, then placed her right hand over her left.

They would have made quite the Ansel Adams photo, he thought, him literally putting all his money into her hands, just to feel the shame contained in her stomach with his own hand like he wanted this. He imagined the *thing* germinating in there already contorting itself away from his fingers before it even knew what he was. Here he was with his generosity for this girl who hadn't thought to tell him she wasn't on birth control, putting him in a position that was not his fault. He couldn't have known what would happen. He could already tell he wasn't going to make his bus to get to the airport on time, just as he could tell she wasn't going to get rid of it.

"We be good family. I always want be a mother," she held each English word tentatively in her mouth, practicing the sounds he had taught her with a tenderness that grated on his ears.

The thing had fluttered then in Yurei's stomach, and his mouth opened involuntarily. She laughed, unable to discern his look of disdain from one of longing. He snapped his hand back, wadded up the bills as he crushed them back into his jeans pocket.

They would never speak the same language.

Anyway, he had told himself, that could have just as easily been indigestion as anything else he might have felt. It wasn't even alive. It wouldn't even know if it was just snuffed out now. She could just take care of it the way a responsible person would. But she refused to just get rid of it.

"I thought the women here did what the men said," he spit in rapid-fire English.

Yurei smiled, cocking her head to one side as if wondering whether he had asked a question or required a response.

Water collected on Benjamin Franklin's face, crumpled up in the now-corpse's pocket.

This was the corpse's purgatory, he decided. A sort of karmic balance for how he had treated Yurei and Airi. For the first time in his life, the corpse realized how ashamed he felt. Now that it was too late.

He sat there, unmoving, for the better part of an hour, before spying the rotary phone with the pad of paper next to it. It was becoming much more challenging to move voluntarily as the corpse sat alone in his deterioration. With a herculean effort, he stood and shambled over to the green stickie notes. The thumb on his right hand would not close around the pen, so he used his left to hold the pen, and his right to stabilize his drooping arm.

What to write? How to write it so it did not read as a suicide note? The corpse shuddered at the thought that he could be remembered for a potential suicide that was never proven or disproven. The mundane horror of mediocrity. A swan song with stakes far too high. These were his final words for eternity to remember him by. His mind flitted from face to face of his colleagues at the firm. What should they know? He could not think of a single thing to say to any of them in farewell.

He thought of Yurei, of whether she might not have stood with a pen in her nondominant hand, trying to come up with a magnum opus in her last moments. Not that she knew what a magnum opus was, per se.

He thought of Airi. And then there was just too much to say. He could fill all the stickie notes on the pad and it still would not be enough space to convey what he thought he wanted to say. If you try to live perfectly, you cannot live well. If you try to die perfectly, you cannot die well.

He clutched the pen with his whole fist as he walked over to the desk, slid out the thin piece of paper and signed his name. He couldn't just leave this out in the open for anyone to find and misinterpret as a way to justify killing himself like a deranged person. The idea was appalling.

He scrawled a few lines on a delicate piece of paper. As he slid the paper into an envelope, he addressed the outside of the envelope, stamped it, and left it on the large writing desk on top of the other mail. Without a word, he stiffly marched himself, pajamas and all, back into his armchair and opened the paper to page six, his eyes fixed on the phrase "8-3 loss."

After a week of waiting for someone from the firm to call, the corpse would hear his daughter's voice on the answering machine. With his better ear now lying next to his right foot and the mildew beginning to rest in the disconnected canal, it was hard to make out the words. Sensation overall had slowed to a crawl, and small blips of errant electricity left the corpse frozen with fragments of his own thoughts as he slowly lost the ability to move his limbs.

And so, when his daughter kept missing him on the phone she would decide to come and check on him like a responsible child.

"Just in case," she would later tell the neighbors who came on the premise of consoling her.

When she made up her mind to come for her first unannounced visit to his practical, down-sized, one-bedroom apartment, he would be sitting here with page six of the Sports section open on his lap, the NPR story playing on loop in the background for effect. When her outdated key would falter in the new lock meant to deter would-be burglars and people he did not know outside the distorted bubble of a peephole, the light below the spider would have burnt itself out hours ago. When the police arrived, after she realized just how responsible she might need to be and would bash in the doorknob with some billy club or device like that, he would be right here in his chair in his flannel pajamas regretting the fact he cremated his wife against her late wishes.

Had she felt it?

The forgotten spider would munch greedily on one of the many flies the corpse had attracted to her newly spun web, watching the scene unfold with no need of one of the neighbors' blue-light TVs.

Death and a lifetime of practical stock choices come for us all in the end, if not in so dignified a manner as chasing down a season-arch villain or serial killer.

How horribly mundane death truly is at its essence, he would muse, his hardened eyeballs like prized marbles watching his daughter's horrified face as she encountered death for the first time. At least Yurei's eyes had the decency to close when he passed a hand over the eyelids. No one would close his eyes and he regretted not shutting them before Airi brought the police. He had always known it would have to be Airi. Who else would come?

"I was just here," she would say to the officer, lifting the letter from the top of the writing desk with. Her name scrawled in his messy handwriting across the front of the envelope. "The other day I was just here for his birthday."

Her fingers would flip the envelope over, allowing a thin piece of paper to fall to the ground from the unsealed envelope. Airi would lean over and pick it up with a stifled cry upon seeing the contents. The blank check had drifted to the floor as though caught and dancing on a breeze. The memo line simply read: "For my daughter."

"He didn't feel any pain," the corpse would hear the fire chief tell Airi. "He probably did not even know he was dead before it happened."

It's sickening, he would think to himself, feeling the last flicker of friction come to a stop in his brain, *how the living lie to comfort each other.*

ALLISON BAGGOTT-ROWE M.A.

Allison Baggott-Rowe (She/her) began writing as a teenager, winning Ohio's "Power of the Pen" twice and advancing to the state level as a finalist both years. Her piece "Wounded Birds" was published by Scars literary magazine entitled Down in the Dirt. She is also a Swarthmore Book Award recipient and a contributor to several literary journals including The Chatterbox, The Goldfish, and Oberlin College's The Grape.

Her written works can be found on her **website**. Currently, Allison is a student at Harvard University obtaining her M.A. in Creative Writing and Literature and is in the process of self-publishing a collection of poetry and short stories. In 2018, Allison delivered a TEDx talk (which can be found on TEDx YouTube channel) about redefining one's life in the face of adversity entitled, "A Fall Does Not Define You, But How You Rise Will Redefine You."

Website: redfeatherreflections.com

AFTERWORD

I could sit here and write the seemingly overused quote by Eli Wiesel about how silence benefits the oppressor, but I think we're beyond that point. The oppressors are winning. They have already benefited from the silent majority while the minority keeps screaming from the sidelines for change, for help, for life.

Today, still, we are burning books, killing People of Color, refusing marginalized and disabled people quality of life, denying women the right to choose, and prioritizing greed and control over human rights.

Cruelty and blatant disregard for life has increased in recent years. Many of us feel helpless, hopeless, paralyzed with fear. And that is unacceptable. People should not fear leaving their homes. People should not have their bodies controlled as if they are cattle. People should not be killed because of the color of their skin, their religious beliefs, or their identity.

We Deserve To Exist.

And we will keep fighting for the equality and treatment we deserve.

ABOUT THE EDITOR
DAKOTA RAYNE

With a lifelong passion for helping others, I started my career as a social worker. For many years, I worked with transient, gang-affiliated, and displaced youth. These individuals had few, if any, options for help. Understanding was rare, empathy scarcer still. I loved what I did, but the things that I saw, and the stories that I heard broke my heart. No story was the same, yet they all had one thing in common: their struggles were misrepresented.

After over fifteen years in social work, Kota decided to combine their passions into Inked in Gray, the indie press that seeks stories that need to be heard. Kota is working on works of their own – blending life experiences with the surreal in The Lessons We Keep, and musings about mental health, survival, and overcoming darkness. Kota is also CFO of a literary nonprofit WriteHive — home of the largest FREE online writing conference. You can find Kota causing chaos on Twitter and Medium.

WriteHive: writehive.org
   Twitter: @inkedingray
   Medium: inkedingray.medium.com

ALSO BY INKED IN GRAY

The First Stain

The First Stain showcases stories with a twist—from haunted visions to heartbreaking omens; vigilante justice to survival amidst metaphysical hellscapes. Enter a fantastical world where karma is Law—merciless and unforgiving. Discover the addiction of memory, and the regrets secreted therein. Within The First Stain, fears become nightmares. Nightmares become reality, and sometimes, the worst that could happen, comes to pass.

These thirteen short stories delve into the themes of death, justice, family, redemption, and ugly truths bound in beautiful lies.

What Remains

What Remains brings together fifteen tales of horror, fantasy, and science fiction. From sacrificing loved ones or oneself, to doing what it takes to keep them alive, these stories shake the soul, rip out its insecurities and flay them on the page.

Careful who you trust. Some quandaries have no right answer when we cannot save what we love most — or when isolation, desperation, and betrayal leave you no choice. Take the journey with us to see *What Remains* when civility, decency, and sanity have all but fled.

Duplicitous (WriteHive Anthology)

Gather 'round for creepy horror stories willed with unreliable narrators and chilling scenarios that put your nightmares to shame. Join our 9 authors in celebrating all that is *duplicitous* and morally gray.

These stories were the top picks from WriteHive's annual horror contest, each a new spin—unusual situations, unexpected twists and unreliable narrators.

All profits go to WriteHive.

Navigating Ruins (WriteHive Anthology)

Change doesn't happen overnight. It starts as a whisper before it crescendos into a roar. One event, one decision becomes the catalyst to change life as we know it. And then we must deal with the consequences.

In this collection, we have ten stories about navigating those ruins to regroup, rebuild, renew. In the rebuilding process sacrifices must be made, reparations must be given, histories must be rewritten. We must do the future justice with our actions.

All profits go to WriteHive.

CPSIA information can be obtained
at www.ICGtesting.com
Printed in the USA
BVHW051253050323
659640BV00013B/528